ISBN: 0-9821196-8-2
ISBN 13: 978-0-9821196-8-6

You can visit us online at: *www.JacKrisPublishing.com*

Copyright 2010 by JacKris Publishing, LLC. All rights reserved. No part of this publication may be reproduced or transmitted in any form or by any means, electronic or mechanical, including photocopying, recording, or any information storage and/or retrieval system or device, without permission in writing from the publisher or as authorized by United States Copyright Law.

Printed in the United States of America.

Ver. 1.0.0-5

Copyright 2010 Soaring with Spelling and Vocabulary Level 5. All Rights Reserved.

Copyright 2010 Soaring with Spelling and Vocabulary Level 5. All Rights Reserved.

Preface

We have designed this thorough program to be user friendly for both teacher and student. The level 5 program consists of this workbook and the **Teacher's Notes/Answer key**.

At the beginning of the workbook is a table of contents that lists the concepts and the lessons that pertain to each.

We have selected spiral binding for our books to ensure that they lie flat when open. The spiral binding at the top of the page provides equal, unobstructed access for both right and left-handed students.

Thank you for choosing **Soaring with Spelling and Vocabulary**. We look forward to the opportunity to provide you with the best tools possible to educate your children.

Copyright 2010 Soaring with Spelling and Vocabulary Level 5. All Rights Reserved.

Copyright 2010 Soaring with Spelling and Vocabulary Level 5. All Rights Reserved.

How To Use This Program

This program is arranged in 36 weekly lessons. Each lesson consists of five exercises labeled **Day 1** through **Day 5**.

For the level 5 program we have selected fourteen list words for each week (for each lesson). Fourteen new words each week should provide an adequate challenge for a student at this level. The list words are meant to provide the student with an introduction to one new spelling concept each week. By gently introducing each new concept, one at a time, the student should not become overwhelmed.

We have found that most children in the age group for which these materials are designed usually need to spend about 10-15 minutes per day on spelling and vocabulary. If your student happens to progress through the material at a faster rate, you may want to consider condensing each lesson into a four day schedule. This can be accomplished in a number of ways, such as combining **Day 1** and **Day 2**, or perhaps combining **Day 4** and **Day 5**. It's really up to you as long as all of the materials are covered during each week.

Please see the **Teacher's Notes/Answer Key** for a detailed explanation (which includes a recommended **Weekly Schedule**) on how to use these materials.

Copyright 2010 Soaring with Spelling and Vocabulary Level 5. All Rights Reserved.

Copyright 2010 Soaring with Spelling and Vocabulary Level 5. All Rights Reserved.

Level 5

Table of Contents

Copyright 2010 Soaring with Spelling and Vocabulary Level 5. All Rights Reserved.

Copyright 2010 Soaring with Spelling and Vocabulary Level 5. All Rights Reserved.

Student's Name: _____

Soaring with Spelling and Vocabulary

Level 5

Copyright 2010 Soaring with Spelling and Vocabulary Level 5. All Rights Reserved.

<<The page intentionally left blank.>>

Copyright 2010 Soaring with Spelling and Vocabulary Level 5. All Rights Reserved.

Date: _____

Long vowels **a**, **e**, and **i**

1. Review Your Word List
Look at the word list below and read each word to yourself. Then review each definition.

List Words		Definitions
maybe	*maybe*	• Perhaps or possible.
donkey	*donkey*	• An animal related to the horse but with shorter legs and longer ears.
complete	*complete*	• To bring to an end. To finish.
discreet	*discreet*	• Cautious and not saying anything that might cause trouble.
athlete	*athlete*	• A person who is in good physical shape and excels at physical games.
staple	*staple*	• A chief product of trade that is widely used by many people.
escape	*escape*	• To break free. To get clear from something.
inflate	*inflate*	• To fill something with a gas or air. To increase beyond a normal size.
hibernate	*hibernate*	• To sleep through the winter season.
frustrate	*frustrate*	• Disappointment. Also, to prevent something from happening.
surmise	*surmise*	• An opinion based upon little proof or evidence.
icicle	*icicle*	• A mass of ice (frozen water) that hangs.
lightning	*lightning*	• A bright flash of light in the sky caused by electricity passing to the ground.
entitled	*entitled*	• A claim or right to something.

2. Take Your Pretest
Turn to the next page to the Pretest section and your teacher will ask you to write each list word one at a time.

Date: _____

Pretest - Lesson 1:   Correction Area:

1. _____   _____

2. _____   _____

3. _____   _____

4. _____   _____

5. _____   _____

6. _____   _____

7. _____   _____

8. _____   _____

9. _____   _____

10. _____   _____

11. _____   _____

12. _____   _____

13. _____   _____

14. _____   _____

Carry-over Words: Correction Area:

1. _____   _____

2. _____   _____

3. _____   _____

4. _____   _____

Lesson 1
Day 2

maybe	discreet	inflate	icicle
donkey	athlete	hibernate	lightning
complete	staple	frustrate	entitled
	escape	surmise	

A. Read each clue. Write a list word in the blanks to answer each clue. Read down the highlighted row to find the answer to the question asked below. Write the answer to the question in the spaces provided.

1. Like a horse.

2. Disappointment.

3. A bright flash.

4. To fill with air.

5. A right or claim.

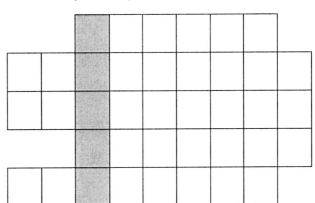

"What did the man think of becoming a steam shovel operator?"

Answer: He ____ ____ ____ ____ ____!

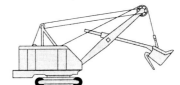

B. Write a list word to match each clue.

1. To finish.

_____

2. Sleep through the winter.

_____

3. To break free.

_____

4. Perhaps.

_____

5. Good at physical games.

_____

6. An unsupported thought.

_____

7. Pointy hanging ice.

_____

8. Widely used.

_____

**Lesson 1
Day 3**

maybe	discreet	inflate	icicle
donkey	athlete	hibernate	lightning
complete	staple	frustrate	entitled
	escape	surmise	

A. Write a list word to complete each sentence. Use each list word only once.

1. The _____ was pulling the wagon.

2. The sky was filled with _____ during the storm.

3. She was _____ to an equal share of the treasure.

4. The knot in his shoelaces would _____ Billy.

5. The bear needed to _____ during the winter.

6. Did the bird _____ from its cage?

7. Ron tried to _____ the flat bicycle tire.

8. The _____ hanging from the gutter fell to the ground.

9. The detective would _____ that the watch was stolen.

10. The train would finally _____ its route.

11. Kristin hoped that _____her sister would play with her.

12. Flour and sugar are _____ foods.

13. Jerry was very quiet and _____ with his advice to Tina.

14. Jacob is good at basketball since he is a great _____.

B. Write the definition from Day 1 for the list word **athlete**.

_____

_____

_____

_____

Date: _____

**Lesson 1
Day 4**

maybe	discreet	inflate	icicle
donkey	athlete	hibernate	lightning
complete	staple	frustrate	entitled
	escape	surmise	

A. Draw a line to connect each list word with its clue.

discreet   To break away from confinement.

athlete   Having a claim to something.

staple   This can happen during a storm.

lightning   It forms in the winter.

maybe   A hunch or quick guess.

donkey   To cause disappointment.

complete   Bears do this in the winter.

escape   To blow up a balloon.

inflate   A food widely used.

hibernate   A professional basketball player.

entitled   Cautious in speech.

frustrate   Something that is all done.

surmise   Kind of like a mule with long ears.

icicle   It might happen.

B. Copy the following sentence. **The icicle quickly melted as the thunderstorms and lightning moved into the area.**

_____

_____

_____

_____

Level 5, Lesson 1 – Long vowels **a**, **e**, and **i**   5

Lesson 1 - Day 5, Final Test   Correction Area:

1. _____   _____

2. _____   _____

3. _____   _____

4. _____   _____

5. _____   _____

6. _____   _____

7. _____   _____

8. _____   _____

9. _____   _____

10. _____   _____

11. _____   _____

12. _____   _____

13. _____   _____

14. _____   _____

Carry-over Words: Correction Area:

1. _____   _____

2. _____   _____

3. _____   _____

4. _____   _____

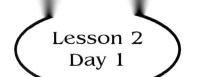

**Lesson 2
Day 1**

Long vowel sounds **o** and **u**

1. **Review Your Word List**
   Look at the word list below and read each word to yourself. Then review each definition.

List Words		Definitions
composer	*composer*	• A person who writes music.
cyclone	*cyclone*	• A violent, rotating windstorm.
envelope	*envelope*	• An enclosure for a document.
vocalist	*vocalist*	• Someone who sings.
mobile	*mobile*	• Capable of being moved or relocated.
impose	*impose*	• To force someone to accept something, such as a new rule.
exposure	*exposure*	• Being subject to outdoor elements or to the public.
immune	*immune*	• To be exempt from or to have a special power to resist.
unusual	*unusual*	• Something that is odd or not normal.
perfume	*perfume*	• A pleasantly scented liquid.
execute	*execute*	• To put something into effect.
compute	*compute*	• To calculate by using mathematics.
unique	*unique*	• To be novel or unusual.
dispute	*dispute*	• To argue or disagree.

2. **Take Your Pretest**
   Turn to the next page to the Pretest section and your teacher will ask you to write each list word one at a time.

Pretest - Lesson 2:   Correction Area:

1. _____   _____

2. _____   _____

3. _____   _____

4. _____   _____

5. _____   _____

6. _____   _____

7. _____   _____

8. _____   _____

9. _____   _____

10. _____   _____

11. _____   _____

12. _____   _____

13. _____   _____

14. _____   _____

Carry-over Words: Correction Area:

1. _____   _____

2. _____   _____

3. _____   _____

4. _____   _____

**Lesson 2
Day 2**

composer	vocalist	immune	compute
cyclone	mobile	unusual	unique
envelope	impose	perfume	dispute
	exposure	execute	

A. Find and circle each list word in the puzzle below.

```
C  E  N  U  M  M  I  E  V  E  G  H  J  K  Q
W  O  Z  Q  O  F  X  N  O  U  N  J  W  N  U
L  F  M  B  K  P  Q  O  C  Q  N  A  O  O  E
Q  C  I  P  O  L  W  L  A  I  W  A  Q  T  D
E  L  O  S  O  W  T  C  L  N  L  P  U  W  I
E  M  U  M  K  S  J  Y  I  U  R  C  B  U  S
K  R  U  W  P  E  E  C  S  I  E  R  L  B  P
E  V  G  F  U  U  S  R  T  X  Q  E  C  V  U
H  E  L  W  R  C  T  O  E  K  F  Q  W  F  T
S  L  R  E  Y  E  Q  E  P  T  K  C  A  N  E
L  B  A  Z  F  S  P  O  E  M  H  T  S  C  N
K  E  U  O  A  D  Q  E  C  N  I  X  G  J  J
Q  N  K  J  T  E  P  O  L  E  V  N  E  C  D
W  G  T  A  Z  X  Z  A  Z  A  Q  H  V  P  O
R  I  P  U  U  X  L  Q  U  N  U  S  U  A  L
```

B. Write the definition from Day 1 for the list word **cyclone**.

_____

_____

_____

_____

Date: _____

composer	vocalist	immune	compute
cyclone	mobile	unusual	unique
envelope	impose	perfume	dispute
	exposure	execute	

A. Unscramble the following list words.

dsietup

1._____

cmopute

2._____

xeeucte

3._____

uqnieu

4._____

eevnopel

5._____

ccyonle

6._____

iosepm

7._____

pfeumer

8._____

cpomores

9._____

mbioel

10._____

valocist

11._____

iunmme

12._____

eurexpos

13._____

uunslau

14._____

B. Copy the following sentence. **The unique composer wrote a beautiful
song for the unusual vocalist.**

_____

_____

_____

_____

**Lesson 2
Day 4**

composer	vocalist	immune	compute
cyclone	mobile	unusual	unique
envelope	impose	perfume	dispute
	exposure	execute	

A. Read the following paragraph and write on the lines below the list words you see.

The unusual composer had a dispute with the unique vocalist on his mobile phone. He tried to impose a rule that she could not wear perfume when she had to execute her performance. She disagreed because she was immune to the scent.

1. _____

2. _____

3. _____

4. _____

5. _____

6. _____

7. _____

8. _____

9. _____

10. _____

B. Finish each list word.

1. p_____

2. u_____l

3. __o_____e

4. c_____r

5. _____ist

6. _____sp_____

7. _____sure

8. _____une

9. exe_____

10. _____mpu____

11. cy_____

12. en_____

13. ____iq_____

14. i_____e

Lesson 2 - Day 5, Final Test   <u>Correction Area</u>:

1. _____   _____

2. _____   _____

3. _____   _____

4. _____   _____

5. _____   _____

6. _____   _____

7. _____   _____

8. _____   _____

9. _____   _____

10. _____   _____

11. _____   _____

12. _____   _____

13. _____   _____

14. _____   _____

<u>Carry-over Words</u>:   <u>Correction Area</u>:

1. _____   _____

2. _____   _____

3. _____   _____

4. _____   _____

Short vowel sounds

1. **Review Your Word List**
   Look at the word list below and read each word to yourself. Then review each definition.

List Words		Definitions
practice	*practice*	• A repeated exercise done to gain skill.
lender	*lender*	• One who loans money to another.
pencil	*pencil*	• A device for writing that uses a dark, non-ink, consumable material for marking.
damage	*damage*	• Injury or harm done to a person or thing.
oxygen	*oxygen*	• An odorless, tasteless chemical found in the air we breath.
customary	*customary*	• Something that is common or usually done.
insect	*insect*	• A bug with six legs and three body segments.
drift	*drift*	• To float in a direction of wind or current.
picture	*picture*	• A captured image of something.
umpire	*umpire*	• One who rules and controls game play.
stunt	*stunt*	• A dangerous or unusual performance.
grand	*grand*	• Great in size or importance.
stock	*stock*	• Tradable shares that represent a portion of ownership in a company.
locker	*locker*	• A storage space used to hold personal belongings.

2. **Take Your Pretest**
   Turn to the next page to the Pretest section and your teacher will ask you to write each list word one at a time.

Pretest - Lesson 3:   Correction Area:

1.   _____   _____

2.   _____   _____

3.   _____   _____

4.   _____   _____

5.   _____   _____

6.   _____   _____

7.   _____   _____

8.   _____   _____

9.   _____   _____

10.   _____   _____

11.   _____   _____

12.   _____   _____

13.   _____   _____

14.   _____   _____

Carry-over Words: Correction Area:

1.   _____   _____

2.   _____   _____

3.   _____   _____

4.   _____   _____

**Lesson 3
Day 2**

practice	damage	drift	grand
lender	oxygen	picture	stock
pencil	customary	umpire	locker
	insect	stunt	

A. **Guide words** are placed at the top of each page of a dictionary to provide an alphabetical guide for finding entry words that appear on that page. For example, assume that a page has the guide words **fast** and **feline**. The entry word **farmer** would not be found on that page because alphabetically it does not fall between these guide words. On the other hand, the entry word **feeling** would be found on that page.

Look at each pair of guide words. Write the list word on the line that would appear on the dictionary page with those guide words.

1. powder   prank   _____

2. pickle   piece   _____

3. grade   great   _____

4. cushion   cycle   _____

5. peace   penny   _____

6. overstep   oyster   _____

7. sting   stone   _____

8. strong   sturdy   _____

9. legal   leopard   _____

10. daisy   dapper   _____

11. dress   drum   _____

12. loan   lodge   _____

13. innocent   insist   _____

14. ultra   uncertain   _____

**Lesson 3
Day 3**

Date: _____

practice	damage	drift	grand
lender	oxygen	picture	stock
pencil	customary	umpire	locker
	insect	stunt	

A. Finish the crossword puzzle.

Across
2. Harm.
5. You write with it.
8. One who rules a game.
10. To float about.
12. To repeat an exercise to learn.
13. It's usually done this way.

Down
1. It's in the air that you breathe.
3. Something that is larger than most.
4. A dangerous activity.
5. A captured image.
6. Somewhere to keep your belongings.
7. One who loans to another.
9. Shares of a company.
11. A six-legged bug.

Date: _____

practice	damage	drift	grand
lender	oxygen	picture	stock
pencil	customary	umpire	locker
	insect	stunt	

A. Write the definition from Day 1 for the list word **pencil**.

_____

_____

_____

_____

B. Copy the following sentence. **The umpire needed to practice refereeing the game in a customary manner.**

_____

_____

_____

_____

C. Underline the misspelled list words in the following sentences. Write the words correctly on the lines below.

1. It was custumary for the linder to use a pincel when figuring out the current price for the stok.

   _____   _____

   _____   _____

2. Without causing damaje, the inseck would driff about in the air filled with oxigyn.

   _____   _____

   _____   _____

Lesson 3 - Day 5, Final Test

Correction Area:

1. _____   _____

2. _____   _____

3. _____   _____

4. _____   _____

5. _____   _____

6. _____   _____

7. _____   _____

8. _____   _____

9. _____   _____

10. _____   _____

11. _____   _____

12. _____   _____

13. _____   _____

14. _____   _____

Carry-over Words: Correction Area:

1. _____   _____

2. _____   _____

3. _____   _____

4. _____   _____

Lesson 4
Day 1

R-controlled vowels

1. **Review Your Word List**
Look at the word list below and read each word to yourself. Then review each definition.

R-controlled vowels are vowels that are changed in sound by the **R** that follows them.

Some examples are the **ar** in g<u>ar</u>bage, the **ur** and **er** in b<u>ur</u>g<u>er</u>, the **air** in st<u>air</u>, and the **or** in sp<u>or</u>t. Notice that **ear** has three different pronunciations in this lesson: the **ear** in b<u>ear</u>, the **ear** in h<u>ear</u>d, the **ear** in h<u>ear</u>t.

List Words		Definitions
c<u>ur</u>b	curb	• To place a limit on something.
g<u>ar</u>bage	garbage	• Trash or discarded waste.
b<u>ar</u>b<u>er</u>	barber	• Someone who cuts hair.
b<u>ur</u>g<u>er</u>	burger	• A slang word for hamburger.
st<u>air</u>	stair	• A structure that is stepped upon with the feet to raise or lower oneself.
b<u>ear</u>	bear	• A furry mammal with long claws and teeth.
h<u>ear</u>d	heard	• Past tense of hear, which is to perceive sound through the ear.
h<u>ear</u>t	heart	• The organ that pumps blood in a body.
b<u>ur</u>n	burn	• To be on fire or destroyed by heat.
l<u>ear</u>n	learn	• To become knowledgeable by practice.
sp<u>or</u>t	sport	• A physical game played for pleasure.
p<u>ear</u>	pear	• A fruit related to the apple that is round on the bottom and narrow towards the stem.
c<u>or</u>n	corn	• A yellow vegetable that grows as kernels on an ear and is attached to a stalk.
h<u>ur</u>t	hurt	• To feel pain.

2. **Take Your Pretest**
Turn to the next page to the Pretest section and your teacher will ask you to write each list word one at a time.

Date: _____

Pretest - Lesson 4:   Correction Area:

1.   _____   _____

2.   _____   _____

3.   _____   _____

4.   _____   _____

5.   _____   _____

6.   _____   _____

7.   _____   _____

8.   _____   _____

9.   _____   _____

10.   _____   _____

11.   _____   _____

12.   _____   _____

13.   _____   _____

14.   _____   _____

Carry-over Words: Correction Area:

1.   _____   _____

2.   _____   _____

3.   _____   _____

4.   _____   _____

Date: _____

Lesson 4
Day 2

curb	burger	heart	pear
garbage	stair	burn	corn
barber	bear	learn	hurt
	heard	sport	

A. Underline the list word in each group that is spelled correctly.

1. curb   cerb   curbe

2. hirt   hurt   hert

3. herde   hurd   heard

4. barbur   barber   barbar

5. corn   corne   cornne

6. staare   stair   staire

7. burn   burne   birn

8. bear   ber   baere

9. lern   learn   leurne

10. garbage   garbagge   garbeage

11. berger   burger   bergur

12. heart   hart   harte

13. paire   paer   pear

14. sport   sporte   spoart

B. Copy the following sentence. **The doctor told him that eating a pear and some corn each day, as well as playing a sport, would be good for his heart.**

_____

_____

_____

_____

Level 5, Lesson 4 – **R-controlled** vowels   21

Lesson 4
Day 3

curb	burger	heart	pear
garbage	stair	burn	corn
barber	bear	learn	hurt
	heard	sport	

A. Unscramble the following list words.

crno

1. _____

htru

2. _____

prea

3. _____

brun

4. _____

brae

5. _____

sairt

6. _____

brgure

7. _____

cbru

8. _____

bbrrea

9. _____

hatre

10. _____

gragaeb

11. _____

sorpt

12. _____

lanre

13. _____

haedr

14. _____

B. Write the definition from Day 1 for the list word **corn**.

_____

_____

_____

_____

Lesson 4
Day 4

curb	burger	heart	pear
garbage	stair	burn	corn
barber	bear	learn	hurt
	heard	sport	

A. Write each group of three list words in alphabetical order.

learn, curb, hurt

1. _____ 2. _____ 3. _____

sport, garbage, pear

4. _____ 5. _____ 6. _____

barber, stair, heard

7. _____ 8. _____ 9. _____

heart, burger, corn

10. _____ 11. _____ 12. _____

pear, bear, burn

13. _____ 14. _____ 15. _____

B. Underline the word in parentheses that completes each sentence.

1. Ray liked lettuce and cheese on his grilled (burger, pear).
2. The (barber, sport) trimmed Mike's hair.
3. Sheila loved to eat (pear, corn) right off of the ear.
4. Argus took the (bear, garbage) out to the curb for disposal.
5. Danny saw the (bear, heart) looking through the garbage.
6. Jordan tried to (hurt, curb) his use of fatty foods.
7. The small girl picked a (corn, pear) from the tree.
8. Phillip's favorite (stair, sport) was basketball.
9. Joy climbed on the (burger, stair) to reach the package.
10. Nathan (hurt, heard) a sound from the other room.
11. Sharon's (burn, heart) was racing after running.
12. The bright sun gave Susan a (hurt, burn) on her back.
13. Carol fell from the stage and (hurt, heard) her foot.
14. Their assignment was to (heard, learn) the new song.

Lesson 4 - Day 5, Final Test

Correction Area:

1. _____ _____

2. _____ _____

3. _____ _____

4. _____ _____

5. _____ _____

6. _____ _____

7. _____ _____

8. _____ _____

9. _____ _____

10. _____ _____

11. _____ _____

12. _____ _____

13. _____ _____

14. _____ _____

Carry-over Words: Correction Area:

1. _____ _____

2. _____ _____

3. _____ _____

4. _____ _____

Lesson 5
Day 1

Contractions

1. Review Your List Words

Look at the list words below and read each word to yourself. Then review each definition.

A **contraction** is a word formed by combining two words. When the words are combined, some letters are dropped. The letters that are dropped are replaced by an **apostrophe (')**.

Examples: they + are = they're
would + not = wouldn't

List Words		Definitions
they're	*they're*	• A contraction of the words **they** and **are**.
wouldn't	*wouldn't*	• A contraction of the words **would** and **not**.
would've	*would've*	• A contraction of the words **would** and **have**.
couldn't	*couldn't*	• A contraction of the words **could** and **not**.
could've	*could've*	• A contraction of the words **could** and **have**.
they'd	*they'd*	• A contraction of the words **they** and **would**.
isn't	*isn't*	• A contraction of the words **is** and **not**.
aren't	*aren't*	• A contraction of the words **are** and **not**.
you'd	*you'd*	• A contraction of the words **you** and **would**.
must've	*must've*	• A contraction of the words **must** and **have**.
don't	*don't*	• A contraction of the words **do** and **not**.
wasn't	*wasn't*	• A contraction of the words **was** and **not**.
might've	*might've*	• A contraction of the words **might** and **have**.
where's	*where's*	• A contraction of the words **where** and **is**.

2. Take Your Pretest

Turn to the next page to the Pretest section and your teacher will ask you to write each list word one at a time.

Pretest - Lesson 5:

Correction Area:

1. _____   _____

2. _____   _____

3. _____   _____

4. _____   _____

5. _____   _____

6. _____   _____

7. _____   _____

8. _____   _____

9. _____   _____

10. _____   _____

11. _____   _____

12. _____   _____

13. _____   _____

14. _____   _____

Carry-over Words:

Correction Area:

1. _____   _____

2. _____   _____

3. _____   _____

4. _____   _____

Lesson 5
Day 2

they're	couldn't	aren't	wasn't
wouldn't	could've	you'd	might've
would've	they'd	must've	where's
	isn't	don't	

A. Write list words that are formed by adding the given words together.

might have

1. _____

where is

2. _____

do not

3. _____

could have

4. _____

could not

5. _____

they are

6. _____

would not

7. _____

is not

8. _____

was not

9. _____

must have

10. _____

you would

11. _____

are not

12. _____

they would

13. _____

would have

14. _____

B. Write the definition from Day 1 for the list word **would've**.

_____

_____

**Lesson 5
Day 3**

they're	couldn't	aren't	wasn't
wouldn't	could've	you'd	might've
would've	they'd	must've	where's
	isn't	don't	

A. Find and circle each list word in the puzzle below. Don't worry about the apostrophes.

```
W   A   R   E   N   T   W   E   Z   C   A   N   H   S   W
W   O   C   T   N   O   D   V   R   M   J   B   E   N   A
J   J   U   Z   U   Y   P   T   J   Y   M   R   N   B   S
L   V   U   L   O   O   F   S   W   W   E   C   B   Z   N
T   F   D   Y   D   C   L   U   Y   H   K   H   Z   E   T
X   V   L   H   G   N   C   M   W   D   X   A   T   W   Y
E   H   C   I   A   S   T   S   I   N   U   Y   E   M   K
L   G   O   V   T   F   P   Y   I   J   Y   O   C   Q   Z
C   O   U   L   D   N   T   S   K   E   I   Q   Y   L   D
K   L   L   X   F   B   N   I   D   G   A   J   H   A   J
T   S   D   U   Z   T   F   E   Q   Y   A   Z   A   X   D
B   H   V   T   E   V   T   H   G   I   M   Z   J   C   S
A   P   E   L   T   E   U   K   O   V   X   A   Z   X   O
R   R   H   Y   K   H   O   N   F   R   E   R   Y   Z   S
S   E   S   Q   D   U   P   Q   L   B   D   E   P   P   Y
```

B. Write the list words that include the contraction for the word **have**.

1. _____   2. _____

3. _____   4. _____

**Lesson 5
Day 4**

they're	couldn't	aren't	wasn't
wouldn't	could've	you'd	might've
would've	they'd	must've	where's
	isn't	don't	

A. Finish each list word. Use each list word only once. Don't forget to add
    apostrophes.

1. mu_____e   2. wh_____

3. w_____e   4. t_____d

5. c_____t   6. y_____

7. wo_____t   8. wa_____

9. t_____e   10. c_____e

11. a_____   12. mi_____e

13. i_____   14. d_____

B. Copy the following sentence. **They're going to the fair, but it isn't as
    much fun as you'd think, so don't
    waste your time.**

_____

_____

_____

_____

C. Copy the following sentence. **It wasn't her fault that they'd be late for
    dinner as they couldn't find their car.**

_____

_____

_____

_____

Lesson 5 - Day 5, Final Test   Correction Area:

1. _____   _____

2. _____   _____

3. _____   _____

4. _____   _____

5. _____   _____

6. _____   _____

7. _____   _____

8. _____   _____

9. _____   _____

10. _____   _____

11. _____   _____

12. _____   _____

13. _____   _____

14. _____   _____

Carry-over Words: Correction Area:

1. _____   _____

2. _____   _____

3. _____   _____

4. _____   _____

**Lesson 6
Review
Day 1**

Review of long vowel sounds
a, e, and i

List Words

maybe	discreet	inflate	icicle
donkey	athlete	hibernate	lightning
complete	staple	frustrate	entitled
	escape	surmise	

A. Write the list word on each line that matches each definition.

1. Perhaps or possible. _____

2. An animal related to the horse. _____

3. To fill with gas or air. _____

4. To sleep through the winter. _____

5. A claim or right to something. _____

6. Cautious and not saying anything
   which might cause trouble. _____

7. A person who excels at physical games. _____

8. A chief product used by many. _____

9. A flash of electricity in the sky. _____

10. To break free. _____

11. A mass of ice that hangs. _____

12. An opinion based on little proof. _____

13. To disappoint. _____

14. To bring to an end. _____

**Lesson 6
Review
Day 2**

Review of long vowel sounds **o** and **u**

List Words

composer	vocalist	immune	compute
cyclone	mobile	unusual	unique
envelope	impose	perfume	dispute
	exposure	execute	

A. Underline the word in parentheses that completes each sentence.

1. The (composer, dispute) wrote a beautiful song.
2. Susan, a (unique, vocalist), sang the song perfectly.
3. Riding a horse was a (exposure, unique) experience.
4. The judge wanted to (immune, impose) a fine for illegal parking.
5. A thunderstorm in the middle of winter was (dispute, unusual).
6. The neighbors had a (compute, dispute) over their property line.
7. The (cyclone, exposure) destroyed many buildings in the small town.
8. Sarah put the letter in the (perfume, envelope).
9. The cell phone was very (dispute, mobile) as it fit into her pocket.
10. The virus was (exposure, immune) to the antibiotics.
11. Mother wore some great smelling (immune, perfume).
12. Congress wanted to (vocalist, execute) a new law.
13. While shoveling snow, Tom was subject to (unusual, exposure).
14. The calculator needed to (compute, impose) the math problem.

B. Write the list words that you underlined above.

1. _____ 2. _____

3. _____ 4. _____

5. _____ 6. _____

7. _____ 8. _____

9. _____ 10. _____

11. _____ 12. _____

13. _____ 14. _____

**Lesson 6
Review
Day 3**

Review of short vowel sounds

List Words

practice	damage	drift	grand
lender	oxygen	picture	stock
pencil	customary	umpire	locker
	insect	stunt	

A. Write each group of three list words in alphabetical order.

practice, locker, umpire

1. _____ 2. _____ 3. _____

pencil, stock, grand

4. _____ 5. _____ 6. _____

drift, lender, insect

7. _____ 8. _____ 9. _____

damage, customary, oxygen

10. _____ 11. _____ 12. _____

stunt, picture, umpire

13. _____ 14. _____ 15. _____

grand, drift, damage

16. _____ 17. _____ 18. _____

practice, pencil, picture

19. _____ 20. _____ 21. _____

Lesson 6 Review Day 4

Date: _____

Review of **r-controlled** vowels

List Words

curb	burger	heart	pear
garbage	stair	burn	corn
barber	bear	learn	hurt
	heard	sport	

A. Match the list word with its definition. Draw a line to connect each pair.

burger   A fruit related to the apple.

stair   A yellow vegetable that grows as kernels on an ear.

bear   A physical game played for fun.

corn   To become knowledgeable by practice.

heard   To be on fire or destroyed by heat.

burn   The organ that pumps blood in a body.

hurt   To have taken in sound through the ear.

curb   A furry mammal with long claws and teeth.

garbage   A structure that is stepped up on.

barber   To feel pain.

learn   A slang word for hamburger.

heart   One who cuts hair.

sport   Trash or discarded waste.

pear   To place a limit on something.

B. Copy the following sentence. **Jenny wanted to learn a new sport to provide exercise for her heart.**

_____

_____

_____

Level 5, Review of Lessons 1-5   34

Lesson 6 Review Day 5

Review of Contractions

List Words

they're	couldn't	aren't	wasn't
wouldn't	could've	you'd	might've
would've	they'd	must've	where's
	isn't	don't	

A. Write the list words that are contractions which include the following words.

have

1. _____

2. _____

3. _____

4. _____

not

5. _____

6. _____

7. _____

8. _____

9. _____

10. _____

would

11. _____

12. _____

is

13. _____

are

14. _____

B. Copy the following sentence. **They must've been lost because he couldn't see the house where they'd been staying.**

_____

_____

_____

<<Intentionally left blank>>

Lesson 7
Day 1

Forming the plural of words that end with **y**

1. **Review Your List Words**

   Look at the list words below and read each word to yourself. Then review each definition.

   When you form the plural of words that end with **y** after a **consonant**, you must change the **y** to **i** and then add **-es**.

   Example: lady + -es = ladies

List Words		Definitions
ladies	*ladies*	• The plural of lady, which is another name for a woman.
puppies	*puppies*	• The plural of puppy, which is a young dog.
libraries	*libraries*	• The plural of library, which is a place where books are kept.
activities	*activities*	• The plural of activity, which is something done to have fun or to relax.
melodies	*melodies*	• The plural of melody, which is a pleasing arrangement of sounds.
authorities	*authorities*	• The plural of authority, which is a person in a position of power or special knowledge.
canopies	*canopies*	• The plural of canopy, which is something that hangs over to provide shade.
injuries	*injuries*	• The plural of injury, which is pain or harm to the body.
factories	*factories*	• The plural of factory, which is a place where goods are made.
impurities	*impurities*	• The plural of impurity, which is something that is dirty or unclean.
memories	*memories*	• The plural of memory, which is remembering.
policies	*policies*	• The plural of policy, which is a rule.
penalties	*penalties*	• The plural of penalty, which is a punishment.
parties	*parties*	• The plural of party, which is a celebration.

2. **Take Your Pretest**

   Turn to the next page to the Pretest section and your teacher will ask you to write each list word one at a time.

Pretest - Lesson 7:   Correction Area:

1. _____   _____

2. _____   _____

3. _____   _____

4. _____   _____

5. _____   _____

6. _____   _____

7. _____   _____

8. _____   _____

9. _____   _____

10. _____   _____

11. _____   _____

12. _____   _____

13. _____   _____

14. _____   _____

Carry-over Words: Correction Area:

1. _____   _____

2. _____   _____

3. _____   _____

4. _____   _____

**Lesson 7
Day 2**

ladies	activities	injuries	policies
puppies	melodies	factories	penalties
libraries	authorities	impurities	parties
	canopies	memories	

A. Finish the crossword puzzle.

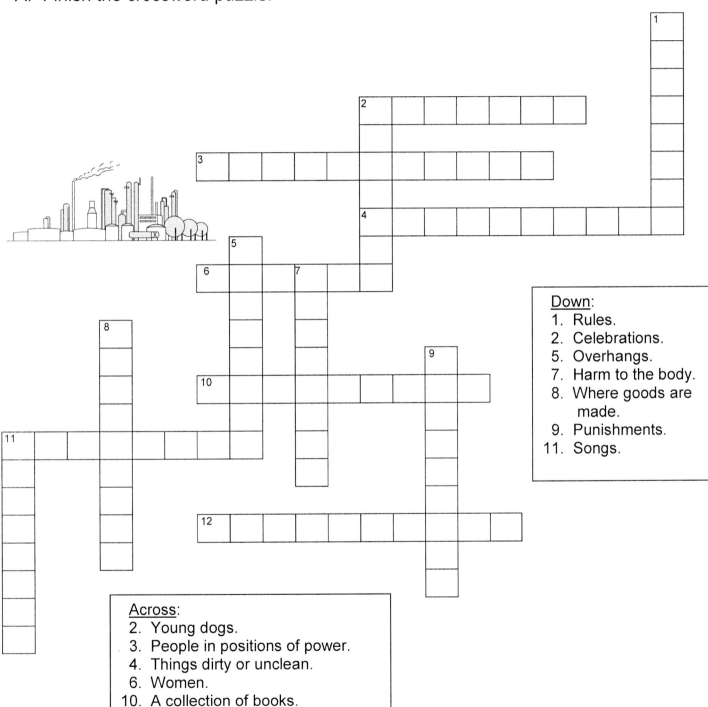

Down:
1. Rules.
2. Celebrations.
5. Overhangs.
7. Harm to the body.
8. Where goods are made.
9. Punishments.
11. Songs.

Across:
2. Young dogs.
3. People in positions of power.
4. Things dirty or unclean.
6. Women.
10. A collection of books.
11. To remember things.
12. Things you do to relax.

**Lesson 7
Day 3**

Date: _____

ladies	activities	canopies	impurities
puppies	melodies	injuries	memories
libraries	authorities	factories	policies
	penalties	parties	

A. Cross out the words that are spelled incorrectly. Write the correctly spelled
words on the lines.

1. (ladies, ladys) _____

2. (penaltys, penalties) _____

3. (librarys, libraries) _____

4. (authoraties, authorities) _____

5. (polycies, policies) _____

6. (memores, memories) _____

7. (canopies, canapies) _____

8. (impurities, empurities) _____

9. (activaties, activities) _____

10. (pupies, puppies) _____

11. (mellodies, melodies) _____

12. (injuries, injueries) _____

13. (factorys, factories) _____

14. (parties, partys) _____

Level 5, Lesson 7 – Forming the plural of words that end with **y**   40

Lesson 7 Day 4

Date: _____

ladies	activities	canopies	impurities
puppies	melodies	injuries	memories
libraries	authorities	factories	policies
	penalties	parties	

A. Write the list word that matches each brief definition.

1. Pleasing arrangements of sounds.

    _____

2. Done to have fun or to relax.

    _____

3. Places where books are kept.

    _____

4. Young dogs.

    _____

5. Another name for women.

    _____

6. In positions of power.

    _____

7. Pain or harm to the body.

    _____

8. Places where goods are made.

    _____

9. Rules.

    _____

10. Hangs over to provide shade.

    _____

11. Things that are dirty or unclean.

    _____

12. Remembering.

    _____

13. Punishments.

    _____

14. Celebrations.

    _____

B. Copy the following sentence. **The authorities have found impurities in the factories that could cause injuries.**

_____

_____

_____

Level 5, Lesson 7 – Forming the plural of words that end with **y**

41

Lesson 7 - Day 5, Final Test   Correction Area:

1. _____   _____

2. _____   _____

3. _____   _____

4. _____   _____

5. _____   _____

6. _____   _____

7. _____   _____

8. _____   _____

9. _____   _____

10. _____   _____

11. _____   _____

12. _____   _____

13. _____   _____

14. _____   _____

Carry-over Words: Correction Area:

1. _____   _____

2. _____   _____

3. _____   _____

4. _____   _____

**Lesson 8
Day 1**

Consonant blends that begin words

1. Review Your List Words

Look at the list words below and read each word to yourself. Then review each definition.

A **consonant blend** is where two or more consonants **blend** together and each letter is pronounced individually. The **consonant blends** that begin the list words are underlined.

List Words		Definitions
blanket	*blanket*	• A layer of something that covers.
progress	*progress*	• To move toward a goal.
special	*special*	• Particular, unique, or extraordinary.
dramatic	*dramatic*	• Forceful in appearance or relating to drama.
grocery	*grocery*	• A marketplace where food products are sold to the public.
glimpse	*glimpse*	• A quick glance.
straight	*straight*	• Not having curves or bends.
splatter	*splatter*	• To splash or spatter a liquid.
scramble	*scramble*	• To mix something together.
class	*class*	• A group of students who are taught together.
crater	*crater*	• A bowl-shaped depression formed by the impact of something.
tranquil	*tranquil*	• Peaceful and quiet.
stimulate	*stimulate*	• To excite or make active.
crumble	*crumble*	• To break into small pieces.

2. Take Your Pretest

Turn to the next page to the Pretest section and your teacher will ask you to write each list word one at a time.

Date: _____

Correction Area:

1. _____   _____

2. _____   _____

3. _____   _____

4. _____   _____

5. _____   _____

6. _____   _____

7. _____   _____

8. _____   _____

9. _____   _____

10. _____   _____

11. _____   _____

12. _____   _____

13. _____   _____

14. _____   _____

Carry-over Words: Correction Area:

1. _____   _____

2. _____   _____

3. _____   _____

4. _____   _____

Lesson 8
Day 2

blanket	dramatic	splatter	tranquil
progress	grocery	scramble	stimulate
special	glimpse	class	crumble
	straight	crater	

A. Write the list word in the blanks to answer each clue. Read down the shaded row to find the answer to the question asked. Write the answer to the question in the spaces provided.

1. Extraordinary.
2. A quick look.
3. Peaceful and quiet.
4. Students taught together.
5. A covering.
6. Moving toward a goal.
7. A place to buy food.
8. Forceful in appearance.
9. A splash.
10. To break apart.
11. No curves.

"When Chris was waiting for his favorite pants to be repaired by the tailor, what was he on?"

Answer:

____ ____ ____ ____ and ____ ____ ____ ____ ____ ____ ____

B. Copy the following sentence. **Be careful when you scramble the eggs, you could splatter some on the stove.**

_____

_____

_____

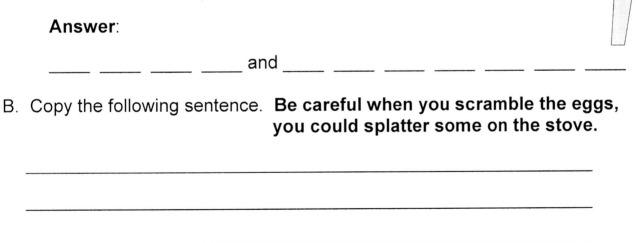

**Lesson 8
Day 3**

Date: _____

blanket	dramatic	splatter	tranquil
progress	grocery	scramble	stimulate
special	glimpse	class	crumble
	straight	crater	

A. Unscramble the following list words.

sitluatem

1._____

curmelb

2._____

cslas

3. _____

gocrory

4._____

secpila

5. _____

scmlaber

6._____

tnrqulia

7. _____

srathgit

8._____

cterra

9. _____

stletarp

10._____

gilmsep

11. _____

dmaratic

12._____

pgrsesor

13. _____

bnkleta

14._____

B. Copy the following sentence. **The special park by the grocery was a tranquil place for the class to relax.**

_____

_____

_____

_____

Date: _____

blanket	dramatic	splatter	tranquil
progress	grocery	scramble	stimulate
special	glimpse	class	crumble
	straight	crater	

A. Write each group of three list words in alphabetical order.

dramatic, splatter, crumble

1. _____ 2. _____ 3. _____

tranquil, class, grocery

4. _____ 5. _____ 6. _____

straight, grocery, progress

7. _____ 8. _____ 9. _____

stimulate, special, scramble

10. _____ 11. _____ 12. _____

blanket, crater, splatter

13. _____ 14. _____ 15. _____

glimpse, straight, progress

16. _____ 17. _____ 18. _____

special, straight, class

19. _____ 20. _____ 21. _____

glimpse, grocery, dramatic

22. _____ 23. _____ 24. _____

crater, splatter, class

25. _____ 26. _____ 27. _____

Lesson 8 - Day 5, Final Test

Correction Area:

1. _____   _____

2. _____   _____

3. _____   _____

4. _____   _____

5. _____   _____

6. _____   _____

7. _____   _____

8. _____   _____

9. _____   _____

10. _____   _____

11. _____   _____

12. _____   _____

13. _____   _____

14. _____   _____

Carry-over Words: Correction Area:

1. _____   _____

2. _____   _____

3. _____   _____

4. _____   _____

Lesson 9
Day 1

Words that end with silent **e**

1. Review Your List Words
Look at the list words below and read each word to yourself. Then review each definition.

When **e** is added to the end of a word, it changes a short vowel sound to a long vowel sound. The letter **e** is usually silent at the end of a word.

Example: rid + e = ride

List Words		**Definitions**
ride	*ride*	• To be carried on or in something for travel.
hope	*hope*	• A feeling that a wish or desire will be fulfilled.
site	*site*	• The place where a building rests or where an event occurred.
stripe	*stripe*	• A line of a different color on a surface.
mope	*mope*	• To be sad or have a dreary state of being.
huge	*huge*	• Very large.
cube	*cube*	• A three-dimensional square.
cape	*cape*	• A sleeveless garment worn around the shoulders.
rage	*rage*	• Very strong and uncontrollable fury.
made	*made*	• Past tense of make, which means to cause something to be created.
scrape	*scrape*	• To injure the surface of something by rubbing against a rough or sharp object.
bite	*bite*	• Gripping something with one's teeth.
slime	*slime*	• A slippery substance that is somewhat gooey and sticky.
pine	*pine*	• An evergreen tree with cones and slender needles for leaves.

2. Take Your Pretest
Turn to the next page to the Pretest section and your teacher will ask you to write each list word one at a time.

Date: _____

Correction Area:

1. _____   _____

2. _____   _____

3. _____   _____

4. _____   _____

5. _____   _____

6. _____   _____

7. _____   _____

8. _____   _____

9. _____   _____

10. _____   _____

11. _____   _____

12. _____   _____

13. _____   _____

14. _____   _____

Carry-over Words: Correction Area:

1. _____   _____

2. _____   _____

3. _____   _____

4. _____   _____

Lesson 9
Day 2

ride	stripe	cape	bite
hope	mope	rage	slime
site	huge	made	pine
	cube	scrape	

A. Finish the crossword puzzle.

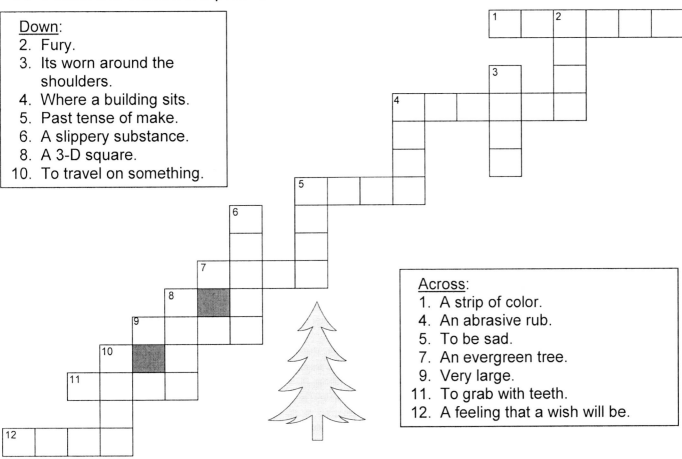

Down:
2. Fury.
3. Its worn around the shoulders.
4. Where a building sits.
5. Past tense of make.
6. A slippery substance.
8. A 3-D square.
10. To travel on something.

Across:
1. A strip of color.
4. An abrasive rub.
5. To be sad.
7. An evergreen tree.
9. Very large.
11. To grab with teeth.
12. A feeling that a wish will be.

B. Write the definition from Day 1 for the list word **site**.

_____

_____

C. Write the definition from Day 1 for the list word **cape**.

_____

_____

Date: _____

ride	stripe	cape	bite
hope	mope	rage	slime
site	huge	made	pine
	cube	scrape	

A. Read the following paragraph and write on the lines below the list words you see.

Kim put on her cape with a stripe. She went for a ride on a horse at the old site of the factory. The horse went into a huge rage and put a bite with slime and a scrape on her toe. Since I was not one to mope, I gave my horse a cube of sugar and had hope that he would head back to the barn made of pine.

1. _____ 2. _____

3. _____ 4. _____

5. _____ 6. _____

7. _____ 8. _____

9. _____ 10. _____

11. _____ 12. _____

13. _____ 14. _____

B. Finish each list word. Use each list word only once.

1. p_____ 2. b_____

3. sl_____ 4. s___r_____

5. s___t____ 6. c___p___

7. cu_____ 8. r___g____

9. hu_____ 10. h__p____

11. r__d____ 12. st_____

13. mo_____ 14. ma_____

ride	stripe	cube	made
hope	mope	cape	scrape
site	huge	rage	bite
	slime	pine	

A. Find and circle each list word in the puzzle below.

```
I  L  H  M  I  Y  I  X  E  P  A  C  E  E  R
S  Q  O  P  K  K  B  I  G  E  F  W  G  M  A
E  P  P  R  I  K  M  Z  T  K  X  N  U  I  X
E  P  E  B  T  N  V  Z  G  M  B  A  H  L  W
I  O  A  M  S  L  E  W  I  P  Q  F  V  S  V
D  I  X  R  A  H  U  Q  I  N  D  E  T  W  K
W  P  N  V  C  D  S  X  F  M  G  W  K  E  H
Y  D  K  P  Y  S  E  C  O  A  E  B  I  T  E
F  D  W  V  B  X  Z  H  R  L  N  T  X  K  R
N  C  R  P  R  F  X  E  C  U  B  E  I  O  D
E  P  I  R  T  S  D  U  E  S  X  D  Q  S  J
H  F  Z  T  Y  I  D  U  Y  Z  R  N  A  I  C
C  R  I  I  R  U  S  V  B  D  F  B  P  F  M
F  L  B  U  Y  Q  R  V  K  T  V  U  H  W  L
P  H  Z  A  G  P  M  L  P  A  E  A  H  W  Z
```

B. Copy the following sentence. **The metal at the site made a huge scrape on his hand.**

_____

_____

_____

_____

Date: _____

Lesson 9 - Day 5, Final Test   Correction Area:

1. _____   _____

2. _____   _____

3. _____   _____

4. _____   _____

5. _____   _____

6. _____   _____

7. _____   _____

8. _____   _____

9. _____   _____

10. _____   _____

11. _____   _____

12. _____   _____

13. _____   _____

14. _____   _____

Carry-over Words: Correction Area:

1. _____   _____

2. _____   _____

3. _____   _____

4. _____   _____

**Lesson 10
Day 1**

Words with oo

1. Review Your List Words

Look at the list words below and read each word to yourself. Then review each definition.

The letters **oo** are known as a **digraph**, which is two vowels placed side by side that act together to make one vowel sound. Notice that this digraph is capable of making three different sounds: 1) the vowel sound you hear in the word **cookout**, 2) the vowel sound you hear in the word **afternoon**, and 3) the vowel sound you hear in the word **flood**.

There is no particular rule to follow in determining which sound an **oo** digraph makes. Practice makes perfect here!

List Words		Definitions
afternoon	*afternoon*	• The part of the day between noon and evening.
balloon	*balloon*	• A flexible item that can be filled with air or gas.
cartoon	*cartoon*	• Drawings that depict a funny short story.
cockatoo	*cockatoo*	• A brightly colored parrot with a crest on its head.
cookout	*cookout*	• An outdoor event where a meal is cooked and served.
flood	*flood*	• An overwhelming rush of water.
foolish	*foolish*	• A decision that lacks good sense.
heirloom	*heirloom*	• A prized family possession handed down from one generation to the next.
kangaroo	*kangaroo*	• An Australian animal with long hind legs capable of leaping. Young are carried in its pouch.
troubleshoot	*troubleshoot*	• To investigate a malfunction.
cocoon	*cocoon*	• The silk covering of a caterpillar while it morphs into a butterfly.
raccoon	*raccoon*	• A small, furry animal with dark rings around its eyes that is active mostly at night.
shampoo	*shampoo*	• A liquid soap made especially to wash hair.
smooth	*smooth*	• Not rough. Having a very even surface.

2. Take Your Pretest

Turn to the next page to the Pretest section and your teacher will ask you to write each list word one at a time.

Pretest - Lesson 10:   Correction Area:

1. _____   _____

2. _____   _____

3. _____   _____

4. _____   _____

5. _____   _____

6. _____   _____

7. _____   _____

8. _____   _____

9. _____   _____

10. _____   _____

11. _____   _____

12. _____   _____

13. _____   _____

14. _____   _____

Carry-over Words: Correction Area:

1. _____   _____

2. _____   _____

3. _____   _____

4. _____   _____

**Lesson 10
Day 2**

afternoon	cockatoo	heirloom	raccoon
balloon	cookout	kangaroo	shampoo
cartoon	flood	troubleshoot	smooth
	foolish	cocoon	

A. Cross out the word that is spelled incorrectly. Write the correctly spelled list words on the lines.

1. (shampo, shampoo)   _____

2. (smoothe, smooth)   _____

3. (afternoon, afternune)   _____

4. (flood, flud)   _____

5. (baloon, balloon)   _____

6. (hareloom, heirloom)   _____

7. (raccoon, racoon)   _____

8. (troubleshoote, troubleshoot) _____

9. (foolish, fuelish)   _____

10. (kangarue, kangaroo)   _____

11. (cacoon, cocoon)   _____

12. (coccatoo, cockatoo)   _____

13. (cartoon, cartune)   _____

14. (cookowt, cookout)   _____

B. Write the definition from Day 1 for the list word **cartoon**.

_____

_____

Lesson 10 Day 3

Date: _____

afternoon	cockatoo	heirloom	raccoon
balloon	cookout	kangaroo	shampoo
cartoon	flood	troubleshoot	smooth
	foolish	cocoon	

A. Use the following code to finish the sentences.

A	B	C	D	E	F	G	H	I	J	K	L	M	N	O	P	Q	R	S	T	U	V	W	X	Y	Z
Ω	☺	⚑	❀	✎	☺	❄	✿	✐	✉	◈	◆	✼	⌘	❖	✈	●	⊙	◷	✪	⊕	✖	⌛	⌇	☎	📖

1. The ___ ___ ___ ___ ___ ___ ___ rose high in the sky.
    ☺ Ω ◆ ◆ ❖ ❖ ⌘

2. It was a very funny ___ ___ ___ ___ ___ ___ ___.
    ⚑ Ω ⊙ ✪ ❖ ❖ ⌘

3. The new ___ ___ ___ ___ ___ ___ ___ smelled nice.
    ◷ ✿ Ω ✼ ✈ ❖ ❖

4. I had to ___ ___ ___ ___ ___ ___ ___ ___ ___ ___ ___ ___ the watch.
    ✪ ⊙ ❖ ⊕ ☺ ◆ ✐ ◷ ✿ ❖ ❖ ✪

5. Tim was done with school in the ___ ___ ___ ___ ___ ___ ___ ___ ___.
    Ω ☺ ✪ ✐ ⊙ ⌘ ❖ ❖ ⌘

6. The ___ ___ ___ ___ ___ ___ ___ ___ was brightly colored.
    ⚑ ❖ ⚑ ◈ Ω ✪ ❖ ❖

7. The water from the ___ ___ ___ ___ ___ damaged the house.
    ☺ ◆ ❖ ❖ ❀

8. The ___ ___ ___ ___ ___ ___ ___ got into the garbage again.
    ⊙ Ω ⚑ ⚑ ❖ ❖ ⌘

9. The necklace was a family ___ ___ ___ ___ ___ ___ ___ ___.
    ✿ ✐ ✎ ⊙ ◆ ❖ ❖ ✼

10. It was ___ ___ ___ ___ ___ ___ ___ to swim in that swift water.
    ☺ ❖ ❖ ◆ ✎ ◷ ✿

11. The ___ ___ ___ ___ ___ ___ ___ ___ was looking around.
    ◈ Ω ⌘ ❄ Ω ⊙ ❖ ❖

12. The fresh ice was ___ ___ ___ ___ ___ ___.
    ◷ ✼ ❖ ❖ ✪ ✿

13. Summer is a great time for a ___ ___ ___ ___ ___ ___ ___.
    ⚑ ❖ ❖ ✐ ❖ ⊕ ✪

14. A ___ ___ ___ ___ ___ ___ was hanging from the limb of the tree.
    ⚑ ❖ ⚑ ❖ ❖ ⌘

**Lesson 10
Day 4**

afternoon	cockatoo	heirloom	raccoon
balloon	cookout	kangaroo	shampoo
cartoon	flood	troubleshoot	smooth
	foolish	cocoon	

A. Find and circle each list word in the puzzle below.

```
G  O  V  F  B  G  J  G  O  T  M  C  L  A  O
B  E  O  B  Y  S  I  O  X  R  O  O  Q  D  X
H  A  V  T  A  F  R  U  E  O  O  O  Q  N  Q
O  O  L  T  A  A  P  C  G  U  L  K  L  G  Z
V  O  R  L  G  K  A  X  A  B  R  O  G  O  I
N  S  P  N  O  R  C  F  N  L  I  U  S  B  E
O  L  A  M  T  O  T  O  I  E  E  T  K  X  D
O  K  V  O  A  E  N  P  C  S  H  R  N  D  J
C  G  O  A  R  H  Y  K  F  H  G  C  N  G  F
O  N  N  N  P  C  S  F  O  O  L  I  S  H  M
C  E  O  E  T  A  R  A  P  O  O  C  T  J  X
N  O  O  C  C  A  R  Z  G  T  S  O  J  O  V
N  A  L  J  N  B  J  W  N  T  O  P  S  X  L
I  F  L  O  O  D  Q  M  T  M  Q  I  B  L  R
G  G  B  K  N  K  A  U  S  Y  R  X  Z  Y  F
```

B. Copy the following sentence. **The flood prevented us from having a successful afternoon cookout.**

_____

_____

_____

_____

Date: _____

Lesson 10 - Day 5, Final Test   Correction Area:

1. _____   _____
2. _____   _____
3. _____   _____
4. _____   _____
5. _____   _____
6. _____   _____
7. _____   _____
8. _____   _____
9. _____   _____
10. _____ _____
11. _____ _____
12. _____ _____
13. _____ _____
14. _____ _____

Carry-over Words: Correction Area:

1. _____   _____
2. _____   _____
3. _____   _____
4. _____   _____

**Lesson 11
Day 1**

Words with **hard** and **soft** c and g

1. **Review Your List Words**
   Look at the list words below and read each word to yourself. Then review each definition.

   -Notice that in some words, like **custard**, the letter **c** makes a **k** sound. This is a **hard c** sound. In some words, like **cylinder**, the letter **c** makes an **s** sound. This is a **soft c** sound. If **c** is followed by **e**, **i**, or **y**, it is **soft**.

   - Notice that in some words, like **glacier**, the letter **g** makes a hard **g** sound. In some words, **gymnast**, the letter **g** makes a **j** sound. This is a **soft g** sound. If **g** is followed by **e**, **i**, or **y**, it is usually **soft**.

List Words		Definitions
dangerous	*dangerous*	• Not safe. Likely to cause injury.
concern	*concern*	• Showing worry or interest.
peaceful	*peaceful*	• Tranquil or calm.
cylinder	*cylinder*	• A round tube.
cymbal	*cymbal*	• A round, thin, brass object that is to be used as a percussion instrument.
custard	*custard*	• A sweet treat made of a mixture of milk, eggs, and sugar.
gymnast	*gymnast*	• One who practices gymnastics, which is tumbling and acrobatics.
geography	*geography*	• The study of the earth's surface.
cookie	*cookie*	• A small, sweet cake-like treat.
giraffe	*giraffe*	• A spotted mammal with a long neck and tail.
tiger	*tiger*	• A large, meat-eating, feline mammal with sharp teeth and claws.
budget	*budget*	• A sum of money allocated for a specific purpose.
glacier	*glacier*	• A large ice structure that usually covers land.
grudge	*grudge*	• A feeling of dislike that lasts a long time.

2. **Take Your Pretest**
   Turn to the next page to the Pretest section and your teacher will ask you to write each list word one at a time.

Pretest - Lesson 11:   Correction Area:

1.   _____   _____

2.   _____   _____

3.   _____   _____

4.   _____   _____

5.   _____   _____

6.   _____   _____

7.   _____   _____

8.   _____   _____

9.   _____   _____

10. _____   _____

11. _____   _____

12. _____   _____

13. _____   _____

14. _____   _____

Carry-over Words: Correction Area:

1.   _____   _____

2.   _____   _____

3.   _____   _____

4.   _____   _____

**Lesson 11
Day 2**

dangerous	cylinder	geography	budget
concern	cymbal	cookie	glacier
peaceful	custard	giraffe	grudge
	gymnast	tiger	

A. Read each clue. Write the list word in the blanks that answers each clue. Read down the shaded row to find the answer to the question asked. Write the answer to the question in the space provided.

1. A mass of ice.

2. Not safe.

3. Quiet.

4. Worry.

5. A sweet treat.

6. A meat eater.

7. Mad for a long time.

8. A monetary limit.

9. The study of land.

"What happened to the egg farmer when he heard the funny joke?"

Answer:

He ____ ____ ____ ____ ____ ____ ____   ____ ____ .

B. Copy the following sentence. **Janet had concern that it was too dangerous to walk on the glacier even though it seemed peaceful.**

_____

_____

_____

_____

**Lesson 11
Day 3**

Date: _____

dangerous	cylinder	geography	budget
concern	cymbal	cookie	glacier
peaceful	custard	giraffe	grudge
	gymnast	tiger	

A. Write each group of three list words in alphabetical order.

cymbal, custard, cookie

1. _____
2. _____
3. _____

budget, giraffe, glacier

4. _____
5. _____
6. _____

cylinder, concern, cookie

7. _____
8. _____
9. _____

peaceful, gymnast, grudge

10. _____
11. _____
12. _____

geography, dangerous, peaceful

13. _____
14. _____
15. _____

giraffe, tiger, cylinder

16. _____
17. _____
18. _____

glacier, giraffe, grudge

19. _____
20. _____
21. _____

geography, glacier, giraffe

22. _____
23. _____
24. _____

cylinder, cymbal, cookie

25. _____
26. _____
27. _____

**Lesson 11
Day 4**

dangerous	cylinder	geography	budget
concern	cymbal	cookie	glacier
peaceful	custard	giraffe	grudge
	gymnast	tiger	

A. Draw a line to connect each list word with its definition.

gymnast   A feeling of dislike that lasts.

geography   A large ice structure that covers land.

cookie   A sum of money allocated for a specific purpose.

grudge   A large, meat-eating, feline mammal.

cylinder   A spotted mammal with a long neck.

cymbal   A small sweet cake-like treat.

custard   One who practices acrobatics.

glacier   A sweet treat made of a mixture of milk, eggs, and sugar.

dangerous   A percussion instrument.

concern   A round tube.

peaceful   Tranquil or calm.

giraffe   Showing worry or interest.

tiger   The study of the earth's surface.

budget   Not safe. Likely to cause injury.

B. Write the definition from Day 1 for the list word **cookie**.

_____

_____

C. Write the definition from Day 1 for the list word **geography**.

_____

_____

Lesson 11 - Day 5, Final Test

Correction Area:

1. _____   _____

2. _____   _____

3. _____   _____

4. _____   _____

5. _____   _____

6. _____   _____

7. _____   _____

8. _____   _____

9. _____   _____

10. _____   _____

11. _____   _____

12. _____   _____

13. _____   _____

14. _____   _____

Carry-over Words: Correction Area:

1. _____   _____

2. _____   _____

3. _____   _____

4. _____   _____

Lesson 12
Review
Day 1

Review of forming the **plural** of words that end with **y**

List Words

ladies	activities	injuries	policies
puppies	melodies	factories	penalties
libraries	authorities	impurities	parties
	canopies	memories	

A. Find and circle each list word in the puzzle below.

```
A  B  V  H  S  K  S  P  I  L  I  P  S  S  U
B  C  A  S  L  E  U  G  I  T  M  O  Y  E  C
M  L  T  Z  E  P  I  B  G  S  P  L  P  I  X
B  E  R  I  P  I  R  D  E  J  U  I  O  P  K
Y  X  M  I  V  A  T  I  A  H  R  C  M  O  L
L  T  E  O  R  I  D  L  D  L  I  I  M  N  U
T  S  E  I  R  O  T  C  A  F  T  E  F  A  R
L  I  E  R  L  I  E  I  Y  N  I  S  C  C  W
J  S  J  E  G  J  E  G  E  W  E  J  G  C  C
R  T  M  T  T  Z  A  S  L  S  S  P  O  H  B
P  J  D  A  U  T  H  O  R  I  T  I  E  S  C
I  N  J  U  R  I  E  S  E  I  T  R  A  P  H
N  M  Y  J  O  U  Z  L  A  M  Z  S  S  G  M
D  Z  C  F  Z  J  L  A  L  O  F  R  R  O  R
I  W  W  D  V  W  L  A  T  T  G  G  C  V  T
```

Lesson 12 Review Day 2

Review of **consonant blends** that begin words

List Words

blanket	dramatic	splatter	tranquil
progress	grocery	scramble	stimulate
special	glimpse	class	crumble
	straight	crater	

A. Write the list word that matches each brief definition.

1. To excite.

   _____

2. To break into small pieces.

   _____

3. A bowl-shaped depression formed by impact.

   _____

4. Peaceful and quiet.

   _____

5. To mix something up.

   _____

6. A group of students who are taught together.

   _____

7. Not having curves.

   _____

8. To splash a liquid.

   _____

9. Food products are sold here.

   _____

10. A quick glance.

    _____

11. Particular or unique.

    _____

12. Relating to drama.

    _____

13. A covering layer.

    _____

14. To move toward a goal.

    _____

Lesson 12 Review Day 3

Review of words that end with silent e

List Words

ride	stripe	cape	bite
hope	mope	rage	slime
site	huge	made	pine
	cube	scrape	

A. Use the following code to finish the sentences.

A	B	C	D	E	F	G	H	I	J	K	L	M	N	O	P	Q	R	S	T	U	V	W	X	Y	Z
Ω	☺	♫	✲	☞	☻	❄	☼	✎	🗄	◈	◆	❀	⌘	❖	✈	◗	⊙	⏱	✪	⊕	✗	⌛	✐	☎	📖

1. The ___ ___ ___ ___ ___ ___ looked like a ___ ___ ___ ___ ___ ___.

2. I ___ ___ ___ ___ he did not ___ ___ ___ ___ after losing the game.

3. The ___ ___ ___ ___ tree smelled nice.

4. The floor still had some ___ ___ ___ ___ ___ on it from the mud.

5. It was time to go for a ___ ___ ___ ___ in Bill's new car.

6. The horse wanted another ___ ___ ___ ___ of sugar.

7. The dog went into a ___ ___ ___ ___ after seeing the cat.

8. The magician wore a ___ ___ ___ ___ while performing.

9. The mountain was ___ ___ ___ ___.

10. Sheila ___ ___ ___ ___ a cake and some cookies.

11. His bark was worse than his ___ ___ ___ ___.

12. This is a good ___ ___ ___ ___ for camping.

**Lesson 12
Review
Day 4**

Review of words with **oo**

List Words

afternoon	cockatoo	heirloom	raccoon
balloon	cookout	kangaroo	shampoo
cartoon	flood	troubleshoot	smooth
	foolish	cocoon	

A. Unscramble the following list words.

crtanoo

1._____

cokouot

2._____

hliemoro

3._____

kngaoora

4._____

rcaonoc

5._____

ccooon

6._____

atfrenoon

7._____

filoohs

8._____

truolbethoos

9._____

sothom

10._____

bllonoa

11._____

coacktoo

12._____

fldoo

13._____

mpoosha

14._____

B. Copy the following sentence. **The cockatoo was holding a smooth, red balloon.**

_____

_____

Lesson 12 Review Day 5

Review of words with hard and soft c and g

List Words

dangerous	cylinder	geography	budget
concern	cymbal	cookie	glacier
peaceful	custard	giraffe	grudge
	gymnast	tiger	

A. Look at each pair of **guide words**. Write the list word on the line that would appear on the dictionary page with those guide words.

1. custard   cymbal   _____

2. damp   dapper   _____

3. concept   concourse   _____

4. ginger   girl   _____

5. pattern   penny   _____

6. given   glamour   _____

7. current   custom   _____

8. guest   gyroscope   _____

9. ground   guard   _____

10. tide   tilt   _____

11. convert   cool   _____

12. bucket   buffet   _____

13. cycle   cypress   _____

14. genuine   germ   _____

<<Intentionally left blank>>

**Lesson 13
Day 1**

Hyphenated compound words

1. **Review Your List Words**

   Look at the list words below and read each word to yourself. Then review each definition.

   - Sometimes the words of a **compound word** are joined by **hyphens**.
   Consult a dictionary if you are unsure.

List Words		Definitions
merry-go-round	*merry-go-round*	• A revolving, circular amusement ride.
mother-in-law	*mother-in-law*	• The mother of one's wife or husband.
T-shirt	*T-shirt*	• A lightweight, cotton shirt with short sleeves and no collar.
well-known	*well-known*	• Something that is known by many people.
twenty-one	*twenty-one*	• One greater in number than twenty.
self-centered	*self-centered*	• To be selfish and only concerned with oneself.
well-respected	*well-respected*	• To be well regarded.
tug-of-war	*tug-of-war*	• A contest in which teams pull on opposite ends of a rope.
about-face	*about-face*	• An abrupt turn-around.
double-cross	*double-cross*	• To cheat or betray.
point-blank	*point-blank*	• At a very close range or distance.
up-to-date	*up-to-date*	• To be current with the latest facts or ideas.
editor-in-chief	*editor-in-chief*	• One who is ultimately responsible for editing the content of a publication.
happy-go-lucky	*happy-go-lucky*	• To be carefree.

2. **Take Your Pretest**

   Turn to the next page to the Pretest section and your teacher will ask you to write each list word one at a time.

Pretest - Lesson 13:

1. _____

2. _____

3. _____

4. _____

5. _____

6. _____

7. _____

8. _____

9. _____

10. _____

11. _____

12. _____

13. _____

14. _____

Correction Area:

_____

_____

_____

_____

_____

_____

_____

_____

_____

_____

_____

_____

_____

_____

Carry-over Words:

1. _____

2. _____

3. _____

4. _____

Correction Area:

_____

_____

_____

_____

**Lesson 13
Day 2**

merry-go-round	well-known	tug-of-war	up-to-date
mother-in-law	twenty-one	about-face	editor-in-chief
T-shirt	self-centered	double-cross	happy-go-lucky
	well-respected	point-blank	

A. Cross out the word that is spelled incorrectly. Write the correctly spelled list words on the lines.

1. (marry-go-around, merry-go-round) _____

2. (well-known, wel-known) _____

3. (well-respected, well-respecked) _____

4. (dubble-cross, double-cross) _____

5. (mother-in-law, mother-n-law) _____

6. (happy-golucky, happy-go-lucky) _____

7. (up-to-date, upto date) _____

8. (tug-ofwar, tug-of-war) _____

9. (T-shirt, Tee-shirt) _____

10. (self-centered, selfcentered) _____

11. (editor-in-chief, editor-n-chief) _____

12. (twenty one, twenty-one) _____

13. (about-face, aboutface) _____

14. (pointblank, point-blank) _____

B. Write the definition from Day 1 for the list word **editor-in-chief**.

_____

_____

Date: _____

merry-go-round	well-known	tug-of-war	up-to-date
mother-in-law	twenty-one	about-face	editor-in-chief
T-shirt	self-centered	double-cross	happy-go-lucky
	well-respected	point-blank	

A. Write a list word to complete each sentence. Use each list word only once.

1. Bruce's _____ had a picture on the back.

2. The _____ looked like a fun ride.

3. Barbara was the _____ of the newspaper.

4. Kristin was always smiling and had a _____ attitude.

5. The instructions with all of the latest changes were _____.

6. His _____ came to visit him and his wife.

7. The play was very popular; it was _____.

8. The boy only cared about himself; he was _____.

9. Tina finally turned _____ years of age.

10. Judge Smith was liked and _____.

11. The children played _____ with a long rope.

12. The soldier quickly changed direction by doing an _____.

13. George shot the basketball close at _____ range.

14. The spy had to _____ his friend.

B. Copy the following sentence. **At twenty-one, Dina fondly remembered her ride on the merry-go-round when she was a happy-go-lucky girl.**

_____

_____

_____

_____

_____

Date: _____

merry-go-round	well-known	tug-of-war	up-to-date
mother-in-law	twenty-one	about-face	editor-in-chief
T-shirt	self-centered	double-cross	happy-go-lucky
	well-respected	point-blank	

A. Count the syllables in each word and write the list words on the lines below in the correct section.

1. List words with two syllables.

_____

_____

_____

2. List words with three syllables.

_____

_____

_____

_____

_____

_____

3. List words with four syllables.

_____

_____

4. List words with five syllables.

_____

_____

_____

B. Underline the list words you see in the following paragraph.

Jerry's mother-in-law bought him a T-shirt that had a picture of many happy-go-lucky penguins playing tug-of-war on a merry-go-round. As the editor-in-chief of *Penguin's Monthly Magazine*, Jerry was up-to-date on his penguin facts and loved the shirt. Since age twenty-one, he was a member of a well-respected group that raised baby penguins. On the other hand, the well-known Mr. Jones was very self-centered and did not like penguins. In fact, Mr. Jones wanted to double-cross Jerry and did an about-face as soon as he saw Jerry's shirt at point-blank range.

Lesson 13 - Day 5, Final Test   Correction Area:

1. _____   _____

2. _____   _____

3. _____   _____

4. _____   _____

5. _____   _____

6. _____   _____

7. _____   _____

8. _____   _____

9. _____   _____

10. _____   _____

11. _____   _____

12. _____   _____

13. _____   _____

14. _____   _____

Carry-over Words: Correction Area:

1. _____   _____

2. _____   _____

3. _____   _____

4. _____   _____

**Lesson 14
Day 1**

More **r-controlled** vowels

1. Review Your List Words

Look at the list words below and read each word to yourself. Then review each definition.

R-controlled vowels are vowels that are changed in sound by the **r** that follows them.

Some examples are the **er** in remember, the **ur** in adventure, the **ir** in confirmed, the **ir** in sapphire, the **or** in abnormal, and that **ear** in appear.

List Words		Definitions
remember	*remember*	• To recall in the mind.
abnormal	*abnormal*	• Not normal.
camera	*camera*	• A device that captures an image.
appear	*appear*	• To become visible.
calculator	*calculator*	• A device that calculates math formulas.
hearsay	*hearsay*	• A rumor. Something heard from someone.
adventure	*adventure*	• An action that involves unknown danger or risk.
agriculture	*agriculture*	• Relating to raising plants and livestock.
contender	*contender*	• One who competes.
surprise	*surprise*	• An act that occurs without notice.
spectator	*spectator*	• One who watches an event.
confirmed	*confirmed*	• To have given notice of approval or acceptance.
sapphire	*sapphire*	• A clear, blue, precious stone.
favorite	*favorite*	• Something that is favored over all others.

2. Take Your Pretest

Turn to the next page to the Pretest section and your teacher will ask you to write each list word one at a time.

Date: _____

<u>Pretest - Lesson 14</u>:   <u>Correction Area</u>:

1. _____   _____

2. _____   _____

3. _____   _____

4. _____   _____

5. _____   _____

6. _____   _____

7. _____   _____

8. _____   _____

9. _____   _____

10. _____   _____

11. _____   _____

12. _____   _____

13. _____   _____

14. _____   _____

<u>Carry-over Words</u>:   <u>Correction Area</u>:

1. _____   _____

2. _____   _____

3. _____   _____

4. _____   _____

Date: _____

remember	appear	agriculture	confirmed
abnormal	calculator	contender	sapphire
camera	hearsay	surprise	favorite
	adventure	spectator	

A. Finish the crossword puzzle.

Down:
1. Most favored.
2. Related to raising plants.
3. To become visible.
5. A risky trip or event.
6. Captures images.
7. Watches an event.
9. Heard from someone.
10. An unexpected event.

Across:
2. Not normal.
4. A competitor.
8. Approved or accepted.
11. Solves math problems.
12. A blue precious stone.
13. To retain in one's mind.

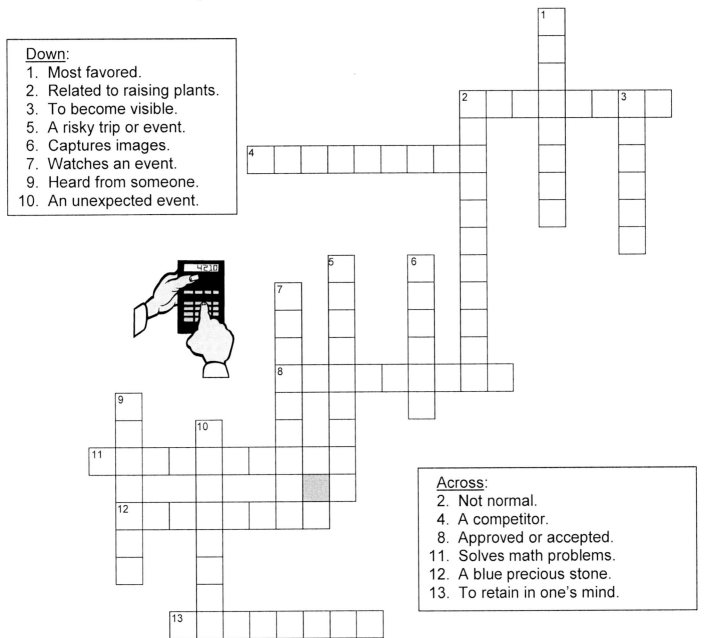

**Lesson 14
Day 3**

Date: _____

remember	appear	agriculture	confirmed
abnormal	calculator	contender	sapphire
camera	hearsay	surprise	favorite
	adventure	spectator	

A. Write a list word to complete each sentence. Use each list word only once.

1. Beverly's _____ takes great pictures.

2. Frances bought a new ring with a beautiful _____.

3. The test results were _____ from the usual.

4. The untrue story heard from the man was simply _____.

5. Jacob could not _____ the combination to the safe.

6. The farmer's livelihood was focused on _____.

7. The treasure hunt was an _____ of a lifetime.

8. Mike used a _____ to figure out the math problem.

9. Robert was scheduled to _____ on the stage.

10. I was a _____ at the basketball game.

11. The boxer was a _____ for the world title.

12. The steak house was Tricia's _____ place to eat.

13. Her vacation plans were _____ by the reservationist.

14. The party was a huge _____ for Grandma.

B. Copy the following sentence. **Her favorite camera took good pictures, but it was abnormal because it also had a calculator.**

_____

_____

_____

_____

**Lesson 14
Day 4**

remember	appear	agriculture	confirmed
abnormal	calculator	contender	sapphire
camera	hearsay	surprise	favorite
	adventure	spectator	

A. Underline the list word in each group that is spelled correctly.

1. remember   remembur   remimber

2. calkulatort   calculator   calculatur

3. saphire   sapphire   sapphyre

4. spectator   spectatore   spektator

5. faverite   favorate   favorite

6. confirmed   confurmed   confermed

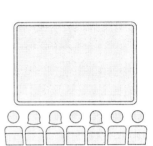

7. camara   camera   cammera

8. apeare   apaire   appear

9. adventure   advinture   advanture

10. surprise   suprise   suprize

11. abnormel   abnormall   abnormal

12. hearsay   hearsaye   hersay

13. contendur   contendire   contender

14. agricultur   agriculture   agricultire

B. Write the definition from Day 1 for the list word **calculator**.

_____

_____

C. Write the definition from Day 1 for the list word **confirmed**.

_____

_____

Lesson 14 - Day 5, Final Test   <u>Correction Area:</u>

1. _____   _____

2. _____   _____

3. _____   _____

4. _____   _____

5. _____   _____

6. _____   _____

7. _____   _____

8. _____   _____

9. _____   _____

10. _____   _____

11. _____   _____

12. _____   _____

13. _____   _____

14. _____   _____

<u>Carry-over Words:</u>   <u>Correction Area:</u>

1. _____   _____

2. _____   _____

3. _____   _____

4. _____   _____

Date: _____

Lesson 15 Day 1

Words with prefixes **dis** and **mis**

1. Review Your List Words

Look at the list words below and read each word to yourself. Then review each definition.

The prefix **dis**, when added to a word, means **not** or **the opposite of**.

The prefix **mis**, when added to a word, means **wrongly** or **incorrectly**.

List Words		Definitions
dislodge	*dislodge*	• To break something free or loose.
misprint	*misprint*	• To print something incorrectly.
disclose	*disclose*	• To reveal or make known. Not covered or hidden.
discomfort	*discomfort*	• Not comfortable. Having slight pain.
misinform	*misinform*	• To provide information incorrectly.
mistreat	*mistreat*	• To be mean or treat something or someone wrongly.
disclaim	*disclaim*	• To deny any connection with something. To not claim.
discount	*discount*	• A percentage taken from the original price.
discontinue	*discontinue*	• To stop doing or providing something. To not continue.
discourage	*discourage*	• To deter an action of another. To not encourage.
misplace	*misplace*	• To put something in the wrong place.
misspell	*misspell*	• To incorrectly spell a word.
miscount	*miscount*	• To count incorrectly.
mischief	*mischief*	• Conduct or action that annoys another.

2. Take Your Pretest

Turn to the next page to the Pretest section and your teacher will ask you to write each list word one at a time.

Date: _____

Pretest - Lesson 15:   Correction Area:

1. _____   _____

2. _____   _____

3. _____   _____

4. _____   _____

5. _____   _____

6. _____   _____

7. _____   _____

8. _____   _____

9. _____   _____

10. _____   _____

11. _____   _____

12. _____   _____

13. _____   _____

14. _____   _____

Carry-over Words: Correction Area:

1. _____   _____

2. _____   _____

3. _____   _____

4. _____   _____

Lesson 15
Day 2

dislodge	discomfort	discount	misspell
misprint	misinform	discontinue	miscount
disclose	mistreat	discourage	mischief
	disclaim	misplace	

A. Read each clue. Write a list word in the blanks that answers each clue.
    Read down the shaded row to find the answer to the question asked.
    Write the answer to the question in the space provided.

1. To break something free.

2. To put in wrong place.

3. To treat badly.

4. To spell incorrectly.

5. To deny responsibility.

6. To stop doing something.

7. To count incorrectly.

8. Actions that annoy.

9. To reveal or divulge.

10. Less than retail price.

11. Printed incorrectly.

"Why did the news reporter want to be the first in line at the new ice cream stand?"

Answer:

He wanted to get the ____ ____ ____ ____ ____ ____

____ ____ ____ ____ ____.

Date: _____

dislodge	discomfort	discount	misspell
misprint	misinform	discontinue	miscount
disclose	mistreat	discourage	mischief
	disclaim	misplace	

Lesson 15 Day 3

A. Draw a line to connect each list word with its definition.

discomfort   A percentage taken from the original price.

misinform   To cease doing something.

mistreat   To deter an action of another.

miscount   To put something in the wrong place.

discourage   To incorrectly spell a word.

misplace   To count incorrectly.

misspell   Conduct or action that annoys another.

disclaim   To break something free or loose.

discount   To print something that is incorrect.

discontinue   To reveal or make known.

mischief   Not being comfortable.

dislodge   To provide incorrect information.

misprint   To be mean to someone.

disclose   To deny connection with something.

B. Copy the following sentence. **Dan needed to discontinue his mischief, as it always seemed to cause discomfort.**

_____

_____

_____

_____

Level 5, Lesson 15 – Words with prefixes **dis** and **mis**   88

**Lesson 15
Day 4**

Date: _____

dislodge	discomfort	discount	misspell
misprint	misinform	discontinue	miscount
disclose	mistreat	discourage	mischief
	disclaim	misplace	

A. Write a list word to complete each sentence. Use each list word only once.

1. Bobby's _____ got him into trouble with Mom.

2. The store had to _____ selling the faulty toy.

3. After getting her tooth pulled, she felt some _____.

4. Randy had to _____ the sword from the stone.

5. The newspaper had a _____ in their top story.

6. Ron tried not to _____ any words on his test.

7. Shelli would either _____ or lose her doll.

8. Daniel seemed to _____ his sister when he was mad.

9. Brandy purchased a sweater on sale with a huge _____.

10. Thomas tried to _____ Eli from jumping off the ladder.

11. Did Bryan _____ the number of apples in the box?

12. The story was wrong and would _____ the readers.

13. Jolie was required to _____ her income to the authorities.

14. The warranty did _____ damage caused by the user.

B. Write the definition from Day 1 for the list word **mistreat**.

_____

_____

_____

Level 5, Lesson 15 – Words with prefixes **dis** and **mis**   89

Date: _____

Lesson 15 - Day 5, Final Test

Correction Area:

1. _____   _____

2. _____   _____

3. _____   _____

4. _____   _____

5. _____   _____

6. _____   _____

7. _____   _____

8. _____   _____

9. _____   _____

10. _____   _____

11. _____   _____

12. _____   _____

13. _____   _____

14. _____   _____

Carry-over Words: Correction Area:

1. _____   _____

2. _____   _____

3. _____   _____

4. _____   _____

**Lesson 16
Day 1**

Words with **pre**, **pro**, and **re**

1. **Review Your List Words**
   Look at the list words below and read each word to yourself. Then review each definition.

List Words		Definitions
precaution	*precaution*	• Care taken in advance.
predominant	*predominant*	• Greater than others in a group.
prepaid	*prepaid*	• To pay ahead of time.
pretend	*pretend*	• To make believe.
profound	*profound*	• Having great knowledge or understanding.
prolong	*prolong*	• To lengthen in time.
provision	*provision*	• Something that is supplied or provided.
protest	*protest*	• To openly dispute something.
proportion	*proportion*	• A relationship between things or parts of things with respect to size, number, or degree.
require	*require*	• To be mandatory.
return	*return*	• To go or come back to an original position.
rewrite	*rewrite*	• To write something again.
reunite	*reunite*	• To come together again.
resolve	*resolve*	• To find an answer to something.

2. **Take Your Pretest**
   Turn to the next page to the Pretest section and your teacher will ask you to write each list word one at a time.

Date: _____

Pretest - Lesson 16:   Correction Area:

1. _____   _____
2. _____   _____
3. _____   _____
4. _____   _____
5. _____   _____
6. _____   _____
7. _____   _____
8. _____   _____
9. _____   _____
10. _____   _____
11. _____   _____
12. _____   _____
13. _____   _____
14. _____   _____

Carry-over Words: Correction Area:

1. _____   _____
2. _____   _____
3. _____   _____
4. _____   _____

Level 5, Lesson 16 – Words with **pre**, **pro**, and **re**   92

Date: _____

Lesson 16
Day 2

precaution	pretend	protest	rewrite
predominant	profound	proportion	reunite
prepaid	prolong	require	resolve
	provision	return	

A. Find and circle each list word in the puzzle below.

```
T  D  P  C  P  S  B  X  M  K  P  S  B  R  W
X  N  S  R  R  Y  T  X  X  R  Z  K  E  Z  P
V  E  C  P  E  E  I  T  O  L  I  W  X  F  R
U  T  D  L  C  D  P  P  B  J  R  H  F  Z  O
X  E  J  N  A  N  O  I  S  I  V  O  R  P  L
J  R  Q  R  U  R  X  M  T  I  E  Z  K  S  O
O  P  N  F  T  O  P  E  I  J  Y  J  V  X  N
D  V  P  I  I  H  F  E  E  N  C  V  H  E  G
N  P  O  N  O  Q  R  O  J  V  A  O  U  W  W
N  N  R  S  N  I  N  K  R  G  L  N  Z  Y  R
R  Y  K  E  U  G  G  G  U  P  L  O  T  Z  G
U  M  P  Q  P  R  O  T  E  S  T  V  S  Z  V
T  E  E  M  C  A  L  R  E  T  I  N  U  E  R
E  R  O  Q  X  L  I  W  V  W  A  C  R  C  R
R  H  M  E  B  I  Y  D  H  M  D  M  U  L  X
```

B. Write the definition from Day 1 for the list word **prolong**.

_____

_____

_____

Date: _____

**Lesson 16
Day 3**

precaution	pretend	protest	rewrite
predominant	profound	proportion	reunite
prepaid	prolong	require	resolve
	provision	return	

A. Underline the list word in each group that is spelled correctly.

1. pre-caution   precaution   precation

2. reeunite   reunite   reunyte

3. protest   proteste   proetest

4. pre-paid   prepade   prepaid

5. reqire   require   requiree

6. reright   re-write   rewrite

7. pretend   pretende   preetend

8. proportion   proportien   proportian

9. predomanante   predominant   predomininte

10. prolong   prolonge   prollong

11. profound   profownd   profond

12. provisian   provision   provisione

13. resolve   resolv   resollve

14. retuern   retturn   return

B. Copy the following sentence. **As a precaution, the politician had to return the speech to his speechwriter and require a rewrite.**

_____

_____

_____

_____

_____

Level 5, Lesson 16 – Words with **pre**, **pro**, and **re**   94

Date: _____

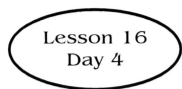

Lesson 16
Day 4

precaution	pretend	protest	rewrite
predominant	profound	proportion	reunite
prepaid	prolong	require	resolve
	provision	return	

A. Use the following code to finish the sentences.

A	B	C	D	E	F	G	H	I	J	K	L	M	N	O	P	Q	R	S	T	U	V	W	X	Y	Z
Ω	☺	ꋊ	⚙	👎	☹	❄	✿	✏	▱	◈	◆	✿	⌘	❖	✈	🌢	⊙	🕐	✪	⊕	✖	⌛	ࣷ	☎	📖

1. The group wanted to ___ ___ ___ ___ ___ ___ ___ the new taxes.
   ✈ ⊙ ❖ ✪ 👎 🕐 ✪

2. Todd ___ ___ ___ ___ ___ ___ ___ for six more months of his policy.
   ✈ ⊙ 👎 ✈ Ω ✏ ⚙

3. The ___ ___ ___ ___ ___ ___ ___ ___ ___ ___ ___ dog is the leader.
   ✈ ⊙ 👎 ⚙ ❖ ✿ ✏ ⌘ Ω ⌘ ✪

4. The ___ ___ ___ ___ ___ ___ ___ ___ ___ ___ of apples to pears was equal.
   ✈ ⊙ ❖ ✈ ❖ ⊙ ✪ ✏ ❖ ⌘

5. Ellen wanted to ___ ___ ___ ___ ___ ___ ___ with her old friend.
   ⊙ 👎 ⊕ ⌘ ✏ ✪ 👎

6. They took every ___ ___ ___ ___ ___ ___ ___ ___ ___ ___ to save money.
   ✈ ⊙ 👎 ꋊ Ω ⊕ ✪ ✏ ❖ ⌘

7. Darrin had to only ___ ___ ___ ___ ___ ___ ___ to sing the song.
   ✈ ⊙ 👎 ✪ 👎 ⌘ ⚙

8. Ed had a ___ ___ ___ ___ ___ ___ ___ ___ thought during the debate.
   ✈ ⊙ ❖ ☹ ❖ ⊕ ⌘ ⚙

9. Allan had to ___ ___ ___ ___ ___ ___ ___ his term paper.
   ⊙ 👎 ⌛ ⊙ ✏ ✪ 👎

10. The contract had a ___ ___ ___ ___ ___ ___ ___ ___ ___ that he disliked.
    ✈ ⊙ ❖ ✖ ✏ 🕐 ✏ ❖ ⌘

11. Buzz wanted to ___ ___ ___ ___ ___ ___ ___ his time on the fun ride.
    ✈ ⊙ ❖ ◆ ❖ ⌘ ❄

12. They needed to ___ ___ ___ ___ ___ ___ ___ their conflict.
    ⊙ 👎 🕐 ❖ ◆ ✖ 👎

13. Marty had to ___ ___ ___ ___ ___ ___ the book to the library.
    ⊙ 👎 ✪ ⊕ ⊙ ⌘

14. The law would ___ ___ ___ ___ ___ ___ ___ cars to slow down.
    ⊙ 👎 🌢 ⊕ ✏ ⊙ 👎

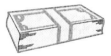

Date: _____

Lesson 16 - Day 5, Final Test   <u>Correction Area:</u>

1. _____   _____

2. _____   _____

3. _____   _____

4. _____   _____

5. _____   _____

6. _____   _____

7. _____   _____

8. _____   _____

9. _____   _____

10. _____ _____

11. _____ _____

12. _____ _____

13. _____ _____

14. _____ _____

<u>Carry-over Words:</u>   <u>Correction Area:</u>

1. _____   _____

2. _____   _____

3. _____   _____

4. _____   _____

Lesson 17 Day 1

Words that mean **full**

1. **Review Your List Words**
   Look at the list words below and read each word to yourself. Then review each definition.

   Each of the words below has the same or similar meaning to the word **full**.

List Words		Definitions
brimming	*brimming*	• Full to the top of the brim of something.
saturated	*saturated*	• To fully soak something to the maximum extent.
bursting	*bursting*	• To be full to the point of breaking open.
replete	*replete*	• To be complete or full of something.
complete	*complete*	• No part is lacking. Total or entirely.
plentiful	*plentiful*	• Abundant. Available in large numbers.
teeming	*teeming*	• To be full of things, especially living things.
crowded	*crowded*	• Filled near or to capacity.
overflowing	*overflowing*	• To be filled beyond capacity.
congested	*congested*	• Crowded to excess.
gorged	*gorged*	• To eat until one is extremely full.
filled	*filled*	• To make full.
stuffed	*stuffed*	• To cram full.
stocked	*stocked*	• Furnished or filled with more than enough.

2. **Take Your Pretest**
   Turn to the next page to the Pretest section and your teacher will ask you to write each list word one at a time.

Pretest - Lesson 17:   Correction Area:

1. _____   _____

2. _____   _____

3. _____   _____

4. _____   _____

5. _____   _____

6. _____   _____

7. _____   _____

8. _____   _____

9. _____   _____

10. _____   _____

11. _____   _____

12. _____   _____

13. _____   _____

14. _____   _____

Carry-over Words: Correction Area:

1. _____   _____

2. _____   _____

3. _____   _____

4. _____   _____

Lesson 17
Day 2

brimming	replete	crowded	filled
saturated	complete	overflowing	stuffed
bursting	plentiful	congested	stocked
	teeming	gorged	

A. Cross out the word that is spelled incorrectly. Write the correctly spelled words on the lines.

1. (overflowing, ovurflowing) _____

2. (stokked, stocked) _____

3. (crouded, crowded) _____

4. (saterated, saturated) _____

5. (briming, brimming) _____

6. (replete, repleat) _____

7. (tieming, teeming) _____

8. (conjested, congested) _____

9. (gordged, gorged) _____

10. (bersting, bursting) _____

11. (complete, compleat) _____

12. (plentiful, plentful) _____

13. (filled, philled) _____

14. (stufed, stuffed) _____

B. Write the definition from Day 1 for the list word **bursting**.

_____

_____

Date: _____

brimming	replete	crowded	filled
saturated	complete	overflowing	stuffed
bursting	plentiful	congested	stocked
	teeming	gorged	

A. Unscramble the following list words.

cotednges

1._____

flldei

2._____

cmolpeet

3._____

ofloverwing

4._____

relpeet

5._____

sotkcde

6._____

grgdoe

7._____

bmrimnig

8._____

tmeeign

9._____

cdrwode

10._____

brsunigt

11._____

pnetliulf

12._____

sfedtuf

13._____

starutaed

14._____

B. Copy the following sentence. **The lake was teeming with fish because it was fully stocked with bass and catfish.**

_____

_____

_____

_____

Lesson 17
Day 4

Date: _____

brimming	replete	crowded	filled
saturated	complete	overflowing	stuffed
bursting	plentiful	congested	stocked
	teeming	gorged	

A. Write each group of three list words in alphabetical order.

overflowing, brimming, filled

1. _____   2. _____   3. _____

saturated, congested, stocked

4. _____   5. _____   6. _____

bursting, gorged, crowded

7. _____   8. _____   9. _____

stuffed, replete, plentiful

10. _____   11. _____   12. _____

teeming, complete, overflowing

13. _____   14. _____   15. _____

B. Write the definition from Day 1 for the list word **saturated**.

_____

_____

C. Write the definition from Day 1 for the list word **crowded**.

_____

_____

Lesson 17 - Day 5, Final Test   Correction Area:

Date: _____

1. _____   _____

2. _____   _____

3. _____   _____

4. _____   _____

5. _____   _____

6. _____   _____

7. _____   _____

8. _____   _____

9. _____   _____

10. _____   _____

11. _____   _____

12. _____   _____

13. _____   _____

14. _____   _____

Carry-over Words: Correction Area:

1. _____   _____

2. _____   _____

3. _____   _____

4. _____   _____

Lesson 18 Review Day 1

Review of hyphenated compound words

List Words

merry-go-round	well-known	tug-of-war	up-to-date
mother-in-law	twenty-one	about-face	editor-in-chief
T-shirt	self-centered	double-cross	happy-go-lucky
	well-respected	point-blank	

A. Write each group of three list words in alphabetical order.

editor-in-chief, double-cross, T-shirt

1. _____ 2. _____ 3. _____

twenty-one, point-blank, mother-in-law

4. _____ 5. _____ 6. _____

merry-go-round, well-known, about-face

7. _____ 8. _____ 9. _____

up-to-date, happy-go-lucky, self-centered

10. _____ 11. _____ 12. _____

well-respected, T-shirt, double-cross

13. _____ 14. _____ 15. _____

point-blank, tug-of-war, twenty-one

16. _____ 17. _____ 18. _____

mother-in-law, merry-go-round, editor-in-chief

19. _____ 20. _____ 21. _____

well-known, tug-of-war, well-respected

22. _____ 23. _____ 24. _____

double-cross, about-face, T-shirt

25. _____ 26. _____ 27. _____

Review of more
r-controlled vowels

List Words

remember	appear	adventure	surprise
abnormal	calculator	agriculture	spectator
camera	hearsay	contender	confirmed
	sapphire	favorite	

A. Read each clue. Write a list word in the blanks to answer each clue. Write the letters from the shaded cells in order in the spaces below to find the answer to the question asked.

1. A rumor.

2. Solves a math problem.

3. Not normal.

4. A competitor.

5. Approved or accepted.

6. Preferred over all others.

7. Action of unknown risk.

8. One who watches.

9. Sudden unexpected act.

10. Related to farming.

11. A pretty, blue stone.

"The baker was doing well. What was he making?"

Answer:

____ ____ ____ ____   ____ ____ ____ ____   ____ ____ ____ ____ ____ .

Lesson 18
Review
Day 3

Review of words with prefixes **dis** and **mis**

List Words

dislodge	discomfort	discount	misspell
misprint	misinform	discontinue	miscount
disclose	mistreat	discourage	mischief
	disclaim	misplace	

A. Find and circle each list word in the puzzle below.

```
E  L  D  V  V  O  E  T  N  T  O  Z  E  V  T
P  U  G  I  N  I  A  C  U  U  E  U  S  E  R
M  P  N  U  S  E  P  U  A  G  D  D  O  I  O
O  I  Y  I  R  L  M  A  A  L  L  R  L  I  F
R  C  S  T  T  Z  O  R  Z  L  P  B  C  S  M
A  N  S  C  I  N  U  D  O  Y  N  S  S  B  O
M  I  D  O  O  O  M  G  R  V  D  I  T  C
M  X  B  N  C  U  I  C  L  E  X  I  D  M  S
C  L  T  S  Z  S  N  K  S  H  B  S  W  I  I
M  H  I  V  P  J  S  T  Q  I  X  C  B  S  D
D  D  V  R  C  M  D  I  F  I  D  L  J  C  S
C  B  I  T  N  U  O  C  S  I  D  A  E  H  N
C  N  M  I  S  S  P  E  L  L  V  I  Y  I  E
T  O  M  A  G  Y  W  O  R  S  M  M  Y  E  X
M  I  S  I  N  F  O  R  M  Z  G  H  G  F  Y
```

Lesson 18
Review
Day 4

Date: _____

Review of words with
pre, pro, and re

List Words

precaution	pretend	protest	rewrite
predominant	profound	proportion	reunite
prepaid	prolong	require	resolve
	provision	return	

A. Underline the list word in each sentence that is spelled incorrectly.

1. As a pre-caution, they stayed away from the snake.
2. The cousins would reunight at the family reunion.
3. The actor tended to proelong the end of the play.
4. Matt and Violet worked together to resollve the math problem.
5. Dalana prepayd her college tuition.
6. The angry group wanted to proteste the closure of the factory.
7. The proportian of students to teachers was about right.
8. Brian had a profond thought as he pondered the question asked.
9. Margaret simply had to prettend to watch the movie.
10. The rules would reqire that he uses a round paddle to play ping-pong.
11. The predomanant investor was from the big city.
12. The contract had a provison that it would terminate in one year.
13. Did Angela returnn later with several friends?
14. William had to rewright his letter to his cousin.

B. Correctly write the list words from above in order.

1._____   2._____

3._____   4._____

5._____   6._____

7._____   8._____

9._____   10._____

11._____   12._____

13._____   14._____

Level 5, Review of Lessons 13-17

106

Lesson 18
Review
Day 5

Review of words that mean **full**

List Words

brimming	replete	crowded	filled
saturated	complete	overflowing	stuffed
bursting	plentiful	congested	stocked
	teeming	gorged	

A. Underline the list word in each group that is spelled correctly.

1. bursting   bersting   bearsting

2. temeing   teeming   teiming

3. repleat   reeplete   replete

4. briming   briiming   brimming

5. gorged   gorjed   gorrged

6. complete   compleet   compleat

7. saterated   saturated   satturated

8. stoked   stocked   stocced

9. conjested   congested   cungested

10. plentiful   plintiful   plentyful

11. stuffed   stufed   stuft

12. overfloweng   ovurflowing   overflowing

13. filld   fillt   filled

14. crowdid   crowded   crouded

<<This page intentionally left blank>>

Date: _____

Words that end with **ed**, **er**, and **ing**

1. Review Your List Words

Look at the list words below and read each word to yourself. Then review each definition.

List Words		**Definitions**
fulfilled	*fulfilled*	• To have been satisfied or completed.
abandoned	*abandoned*	• Left empty or unused.
confessed	*confessed*	• To have admitted to something.
scattered	*scattered*	• To have separate or moved in different directions.
laborer	*laborer*	• A person who does hard physical work.
dreaming	*dreaming*	• Having a series of mental images while asleep.
protecting	*protecting*	• Keeping something safe from harm or damage.
bartering	*bartering*	• Exchanging goods or services without using money.
fastening	*fastening*	• To hold something together or in place.
wandering	*wandering*	• Moving about without any meaning.
launcher	*launcher*	• One that projects something into the air with force.
commander	*commander*	• A person who commands.
messenger	*messenger*	• One who delivers a message or information.
lighter	*lighter*	• Something that provides a flame.

2. Take Your Pretest

Turn to the next page to the Pretest section and your teacher will ask you to write each list word one at a time.

Date: _____

Correction Area:

1. _____   _____

2. _____   _____

3. _____   _____

4. _____   _____

5. _____   _____

6. _____   _____

7. _____   _____

8. _____   _____

9. _____   _____

10. _____   _____

11. _____   _____

12. _____   _____

13. _____   _____

14. _____   _____

Carry-over Words: Correction Area:

1. _____   _____

2. _____   _____

3. _____   _____

4. _____   _____

**Lesson 19
Day 2**

fulfilled	scattered	bartering	commander
abandoned	laborer	fastening	messenger
confessed	dreaming	wandering	lighter
	protecting	launcher	

A. **Guide words** are placed at the top of each page of a dictionary to provide an alphabetical guide for finding entry words that appear on that page. For example, assume that a page has the guide words **fast** and **feline**. The entry word **farmer** would not be found on that page because alphabetically it does not fall between these **guide words**. On the other hand, the entry word **feeling** would be found on that page.

Look at each pair of **guide words**. Write the list word on the line that would appear on the dictionary page with those **guide words**.

1. fugitive   fun   _____

2. abacus   ability   _____

3. scant   scent   _____

4. barrel   base   _____

5. drastic   dredge   _____

6. property   proud   _____

7. fast   fate   _____

8. merit   metal   _____

9. cobra   cope   _____

10. laugh   lava   _____

11. cloud   confident   _____

12. lift   like   _____

13. walrus   warden   _____

14. label   lady   _____

Lesson 19
Day 3

fulfilled	scattered	bartering	commander
abandoned	laborer	fastening	messenger
confessed	dreaming	wandering	lighter
	protecting	launcher	

A. Read the following paragraphs and write on the lines below the list words you see.

The laborer accidentally scattered his lunch like a rocket launcher. The messenger felt sorry for him and fulfilled his hunger by bartering his sandwich for the hungry man's grill lighter.

1. _____   2. _____

3. _____   4. _____

5. _____   6. _____

7. _____

Protecting his commander who was dreaming, the thief finally abandoned his story and confessed to the crime of not fastening the gate while cows were wandering about.

8. _____   9. _____

10. _____   11. _____

12. _____   13. _____

14. _____

B. Copy the following sentence. **The messenger was wandering about the city with a package that was to be delivered to the laborer.**

_____

_____

_____

_____

Lesson 19
Day 4

fulfilled	scattered	bartering	commander
abandoned	laborer	fastening	messenger
confessed	dreaming	wandering	lighter
	protecting	launcher	

A. Underline the word in parentheses that completes each sentence. Write the correctly spelled list words on the lines below

1. Alice (fulfilled, fullfilled) her promise to Ralph.
2. The teacher (scatered, scattered) the chalk on the ground.
3. Last night I was (dreaming, dreeming) about swimming in the ocean.
4. Dale (confessed, confesed) to eating all of the ice cream.
5. Gary was a bike (mesenger, messenger) in New York City.
6. Elizabeth used her (lighter, leiter) to start the fire.
7. They were (whandering, wandering) around the amusement park.
8. Raymond was a (laberer, laborer) in the coalmine.
9. Janet was (protecting, protechting) her sore arm.
10. They had (abandened, abandoned) the old trash can.
11. Steven was (bartering, bartring) with the merchant for a new necklace.
12. Jerod was (fastening, fastning) his coat as he left the house.
13. The (launcher, luncher) released the rocket into space.
14. The (comandur, commander) of the ship blew the whistle.

1. _____   2. _____

3. _____   4. _____

5. _____   6. _____

7. _____   8. _____

9. _____   10. _____

11. _____   12. _____

13. _____   14. _____

B. Write the definition from Day 1 for the list word **messenger**.

_____

_____

Lesson 19 - Day 5, Final Test   <u>Correction Area</u>:

1. _____   _____

2. _____   _____

3. _____   _____

4. _____   _____

5. _____   _____

6. _____   _____

7. _____   _____

8. _____   _____

9. _____   _____

10. _____   _____

11. _____   _____

12. _____   _____

13. _____   _____

14. _____   _____

<u>Carry-over Words</u>:   <u>Correction Area</u>:

1. _____   _____

2. _____   _____

3. _____   _____

4. _____   _____

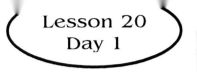

Lesson 20
Day 1

More words that end with
ed, er, and ing

1. Review Your List Words

Look at the list words below and read each word to yourself. Then review each definition.

When you add **ed**, **er**, or **ing** to a word that ends with **e**, you must drop the final **e** and then add **ed**, **er**, or **ing**.

Examples: educate + ed = educated
lecture + er = lecturer
validate + ing = validating

List Words		**Definitions**
duplicated	*duplicated*	• To have copied from an original.
educated	*educated*	• To have received an education.
lecturer	*lecturer*	• One who teaches by speaking.
manager	*manager*	• One who directs and makes decisions.
consumer	*consumer*	• One who purchases and consumes goods.
advertiser	*advertiser*	• One who announces publically with hopes of selling something.
concluded	*concluded*	• To have finished or brought something to an end.
involved	*involved*	• Something that is complex or hard to understand. Complicated.
explorer	*explorer*	• One who travels to discover things.
believer	*believer*	• One who has faith or confidence.
validating	*validating*	• The act of making something valid.
updating	*updating*	• The act of making something current.
simulating	*simulating*	• The act of copying or mimicking.
igniting	*igniting*	• The act of setting something on fire.

2. Take Your Pretest

Turn to the next page to the Pretest section and your teacher will ask you to write each list word one at a time.

Pretest - Lesson 20:   Correction Area:

1. _____   _____

2. _____   _____

3. _____   _____

4. _____   _____

5. _____   _____

6. _____   _____

7. _____   _____

8. _____   _____

9. _____   _____

10. _____   _____

11. _____   _____

12. _____   _____

13. _____   _____

14. _____   _____

Carry-over Words: Correction Area:

1. _____   _____

2. _____   _____

3. _____   _____

4. _____   _____

Lesson 20
Day 2

duplicated	manager	involved	updating
educated	consumer	explorer	simulating
lecturer	advertiser	believer	igniting
	concluded	validating	

A. Use the following code to finish the sentences.

A	B	C	D	E	F	G	H	I	J	K	L	M	N	O	P	Q	R	S	T	U	V	W	X	Y	Z
Ω	☺	♫	✿	☞	☹	❄	✿	✎	✉	◇	◆	✿	⌘	❖	✈	●	☉	⏱	✪	⊕	✕	⌛	✍	☎	📖

1. Harold __ __ __ __ __ __ __ __ __ __ __ the famous painting.

2. Ben was __ __ __ __ __ __ __ __ at the local college.

3. Sue was __ __ __ __ __ __ __ __ __ __ the conductor's movements.

4. The play __ __ __ __ __ __ __ __ __ with a group song.

5. The clerk was __ __ __ __ __ __ __ __ __ __ the parking ticket.

6. They took notes as the __ __ __ __ __ __ __ __ spoke.

7. Cathy was the __ __ __ __ __ __ __ of the hotel.

8. Marcy was a great __ __ __ __ __ __ __ __ of antique plates.

9. The store was an __ __ __ __ __ __ __ __ __ __ in the newspaper.

10. Larry was __ __ __ __ __ __ __ __ __ the campfire.

11. Megan got __ __ __ __ __ __ __ __ in a new music group.

12. Lewis was a great __ __ __ __ __ __ __ __ in the Midwest.

13. John was a __ __ __ __ __ __ __ __ of the soccer team.

14. Is Dad __ __ __ __ __ __ __ __ __ the computer software?

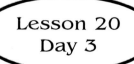

**Lesson 20
Day 3**

duplicated	manager	involved	updating
educated	consumer	explorer	simulating
lecturer	advertiser	believer	igniting
	concluded	validating	

A. Finish each list word. Use each list word only once.

1. s_____

2. ig_____

3. ____ct_____

4. c_____r

5. _____ie_____

6. ex_____

7. _____uc_____

8. _____pli_____

9. m_____

10. v_____

11. c_____d

12. a_____

13. u_____

14. in_____

B. Copy the following sentence. **When he finally made it home, the explorer had completed his simulated journey of Lewis and Clark.**

_____

_____

_____

_____

_____

C. Write the definition from Day 1 for the list word **involved**.

_____

_____

**Lesson 20
Day 4**

duplicated	manager	involved	updating
educated	consumer	explorer	simulating
lecturer	advertiser	believer	igniting
	concluded	validating	

A. Write each group of three list words in alphabetical order.

educated, advertiser, igniting

1. _____ 2. _____ 3. _____

believer, updating, explorer

4. _____ 5. _____ 6. _____

manager, involved, concluded

7. _____ 8. _____ 9. _____

simulating, validating, consumer

10. _____ 11. _____ 12. _____

lecturer, duplicated, believer

13. _____ 14. _____ 15. _____

educated, manager, igniting

16. _____ 17. _____ 18. _____

validating, advertiser, consumer

19. _____ 20. _____ 21. _____

duplicated, consumer, concluded

22. _____ 23. _____ 24. _____

updating, concluded, simulating

25. _____ 26. _____ 27. _____

Lesson 20 - Day 5, Final Test

Correction Area:

1. _____ _____

2. _____ _____

3. _____ _____

4. _____ _____

5. _____ _____

6. _____ _____

7. _____ _____

8. _____ _____

9. _____ _____

10. _____ _____

11. _____ _____

12. _____ _____

13. _____ _____

14. _____ _____

Carry-over Words:

Correction Area:

1. _____ _____

2. _____ _____

3. _____ _____

4. _____ _____

Lesson 21
Day 1

Words with the **sh** sound using **sh**, **ci**, **ti**, and **si**

1. Review Your List Word

Look at the list words below and read each word to yourself. Then review each definition.

The letter combination **sh** is usually used at the beginning or the end of a word to make the **sh** sound, as in the word **sh**oes. The letter combinations **ci**, **ti**, and **si** are usually used in the middle of a word to make the **sh** sound, as in the words electri**ci**an, fic**ti**on, and conclu**si**on.

List Words		Definitions
<u>sh</u>oes	*shoes*	• Coverings for the feet that have a sole.
electri<u>ci</u>an	*electrician*	• A person who installs or repairs electrical lines.
fic<u>ti</u>on	*fiction*	• Something that is not a fact.
conclu<u>si</u>on	*conclusion*	• An ending or final decision.
offi<u>ci</u>al	*official*	• One who has authority to perform a duty or act.
pa<u>ti</u>ent	*patient*	• Showing calmness or tolerance.
confu<u>si</u>on	*confusion*	• To be unclear or mentally uncertain.
ini<u>ti</u>al	*initial*	• The first or beginning of something.
vaca<u>ti</u>on	*vacation*	• A holiday. A period of time devoted to resting.
mis<u>si</u>on	*mission*	• A task to be accomplished.
ses<u>si</u>on	*session*	• A series of meetings.
musi<u>ci</u>an	*musician*	• One who performs music.
spa<u>ci</u>ous	*spacious*	• Large and roomy.
<u>sh</u>arp	*sharp*	• A thin, fine edge for cutting or slicing.

2. Take Your Pretest

Turn to the next page to the Pretest section and your teacher will ask you to write each list word one at a time.

Date: _____

Correction Area:

1. _____   _____

2. _____   _____

3. _____   _____

4. _____   _____

5. _____   _____

6. _____   _____

7. _____   _____

8. _____   _____

9. _____   _____

10. _____   _____

11. _____   _____

12. _____   _____

13. _____   _____

14. _____   _____

Carry-over Words: Correction Area:

1. _____   _____

2. _____   _____

3. _____   _____

4. _____   _____

Date: _____

shoes	conclusion	initial	musician
electrician	official	vacation	spacious
fiction	patient	mission	sharp
	confusion	session	

A. Write the list words that complete each sentence.

1. Her new _____ were made for running.

2. The knife blade was extremely _____.

3. The _____ fixed the wiring in our home.

4. Her _____ thought was to stay at home.

5. Their _____ was to win the competition.

6. After a long summer, the class was again in _____.

7. Pat was an _____ at the spelling bee.

8. Jeremy was very _____ to wait for his sister.

9. The room was filled with panic and _____.

10. The _____ of the movie was a total surprise.

11. My family took a _____ to Hawaii last year.

12. Anita was quite an accomplished _____ on the flute.

13. Roy's story was outrageous; luckily, it was one of _____.

14. Kristin's bedroom is very large and _____.

B. Write the definition from Day 1 for the list word **electrician**.

_____

_____

_____

_____

**Lesson 21
Day 3**

Date: _____

shoes	conclusion	initial	musician
electrician	official	vacation	spacious
fiction	patient	mission	sharp
	confusion	session	

A. Find and circle each list word in the puzzle below.

```
K O S N E U M B N A N M S K E
C Y F X D I C O L O Z U H I V
G K Z F S Z I V I J G S O B A
E X D S I T B S L A E I E F C
F K I D C C U D R R V C S T A
E O B I Y L I S P A T I E N T
N H F L C N K A H B P A T M I
F S P N A O X H L P Z N S V O
B N O U H I C O N F U S I O N
S C Q X L S T L A I C E P S B
F U W Y X S Y I P R A H S C C
F G R V K E C J N M P I L Z Z
T S B E L S P A C I O U S E B
C M W K L Z M A L N C D U X A
D P E L E C T R I C I A N Z C
```

B. Copy the following sentence. **The musician wore his spacious shoes at the conclusion of the recording session.**

_____

_____

_____

_____

Level 5, Lesson 21 – Words with the **sh** sound using **sh**, **ci**, **ti**, and **si**   124

**Lesson 21
Day 4**

shoes	conclusion	initial	musician
electrician	official	vacation	spacious
fiction	patient	mission	sharp
	confusion	session	

A. Underline the letters in the following words that make the **sh** sound.

1. shoes   2. conclusion   3. musician

4. fiction   5. spacious   6. session

7. vacation   8. official   9. patient

10. mission   11. confusion   12. electrician

13. initial   14. sharp

B. Write each group of three list words in alphabetical order.

official, electrician, mission

1. _____ 2. _____ 3. _____

shoes, session, fiction

4. _____ 5. _____ 6. _____

conclusion, spacious, initial

7. _____ 8. _____ 9. _____

patient, confusion, sharp

10. _____ 11. _____ 12. _____

vacation, musician, mission

13. _____ 14. _____ 15. _____

Lesson 21 - Day 5, Final Test   <u>Correction Area</u>:

1. _____   _____

2. _____   _____

3. _____   _____

4. _____   _____

5. _____   _____

6. _____   _____

7. _____   _____

8. _____   _____

9. _____   _____

10. _____   _____

11. _____   _____

12. _____   _____

13. _____   _____

14. _____   _____

<u>Carry-over Words</u>:   <u>Correction Area</u>:

1. _____   _____

2. _____   _____

3. _____   _____

4. _____   _____

Lesson 22
Day 1

Words with suffixes
ful, **ment**, and **less**

1. Review Your List Words

Look at the list words below and read each word to yourself. Then review each definition.

-The suffix **ful**, when added to a word, means **full of** or **having**.

-The suffix **ment**, when added to a word, means an **action**, **process**, or **act** of a specific kind.

-The suffix **less**, when added to a word, means **without**.

List Words		Definitions
improvement	*improvement*	• The process of getting better.
appointment	*appointment*	• The process of choosing someone for a position.
government	*government*	• The act of governing, which is exercising political authority.
investment	*investment*	• The act of investing, which is placing money in hopes of earning a future profit.
bashful	*bashful*	• Full of shyness.
beautiful	*beautiful*	• Full of beauty.
watchful	*watchful*	• Full of vigilance and alertness.
rightful	*rightful*	• Having a just or proper claim.
grateful	*grateful*	• Full of thanks.
cordless	*cordless*	• Without a cord.
fruitless	*fruitless*	• Without value. Unproductive.
motionless	*motionless*	• Without movement.
reckless	*reckless*	• Without care. No regard for danger.
tasteless	*tasteless*	• Without flavor.

2. Take Your Pretest

Turn to the next page to the Pretest section and your teacher will ask you to write each list word one at a time.

Pretest - Lesson 22:   Correction Area:

1. _____ _____

2. _____ _____

3. _____ _____

4. _____ _____

5. _____ _____

6. _____ _____

7. _____ _____

8. _____ _____

9. _____ _____

10. _____ _____

11. _____ _____

12. _____ _____

13. _____ _____

14. _____ _____

Carry-over Words: Correction Area:

1. _____ _____

2. _____ _____

3. _____ _____

4. _____ _____

Lesson 22
Day 2

improvement	investment	rightful	motionless
appointment	bashful	grateful	reckless
government	beautiful	cordless	tasteless
	watchful	fruitless	

A. Read each clue. Write a list word in the blanks that answers each clue. Read down the shaded cells to find the answer to the question asked. Write the answer to the question in the spaces provided.

1. Without movement.
2. Full of beauty.
3. Without care.
4. Unproductive.
5. Full of thanks.
6. The act of investing.
7. Without a cord.
8. The act of governing.
9. Choosing one for a position.
10. Having no flavor.

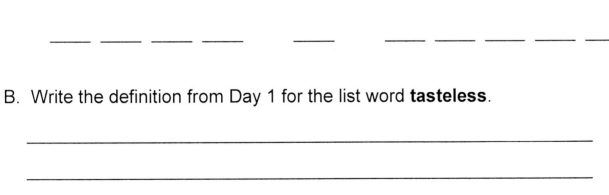

"Why did the girl not want to become an actress?"

Answer: She didn't want to...

____ ____ ____ ____   ____   ____ ____ ____ ____ ____.

B. Write the definition from Day 1 for the list word **tasteless**.

_____

_____

_____

**Lesson 22
Day 3**

Date: _____

improvement	investment	rightful	motionless
appointment	bashful	grateful	reckless
government	beautiful	cordless	tasteless
	watchful	fruitless	

A. Draw a line to connect each list word with its definition.

investment   Money placed in hopes of earning a future profit.

bashful   Full of vigilance and alertness.

beautiful   Full of thanks.

reckless   Having a just or proper claim.

watchful   A system of political authority.

rightful   Full of beauty.

grateful   Full of shyness.

tasteless   The process of choosing someone for a position.

fruitless   Without a cord.

motionless   Without value. Unproductive.

cordless   Without movement.

improvement   The process of getting better.

government   Without care. No regard for danger.

appointment   Without flavor.

B. Copy the following sentence. **Troy was grateful that Nellie gave him the tip to make an investment in a government bond.**

_____

_____

_____

_____

Level 5, Lesson 22 – Words with suffixes **ful**, **ment**, and **less**   130

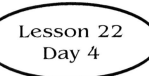

**Lesson 22
Day 4**

improvement	investment	rightful	motionless
appointment	bashful	grateful	reckless
government	beautiful	cordless	tasteless
	watchful	fruitless	

A. Cross out the word that is spelled incorrectly. Write the correctly spelled words on the lines.

1. (goverment, government)　　　_____

2. (wreckless, reckless)　　　_____

3. (beautiful, beutiful)　　　_____

4. (bashfull, bashful)　　　_____

5. (grateful, greatful)　　　_____

6. (fruteless, fruitless)　　　_____

7. (appointment, apointment)　　　_____

8. (cordseless, cordless)　　　_____

9. (motionless, motiunless)　　　_____

10. (improvement, emprovement)　　　_____

11. (tastefull, tasteful)　　　_____

12. (rightful, riteful)　　　_____

13. (wachful, watchful)　　　_____

14. (investment, investmant)　　　_____

B. Write the definition from Day 1 for the list word **investment**.

_____

_____

_____

Lesson 22 - Day 5, Final Test   Correction Area:

1. _____   _____

2. _____   _____

3. _____   _____

4. _____   _____

5. _____   _____

6. _____   _____

7. _____   _____

8. _____   _____

9. _____   _____

10. _____   _____

11. _____   _____

12. _____   _____

13. _____   _____

14. _____   _____

Carry-over Words: Correction Area:

1. _____   _____

2. _____   _____

3. _____   _____

4. _____   _____

Date: _____

Words with suffixes
ness, **ist**, and **ant**

1. **Review Your List Words**
Look at the list words below and read each word to yourself. Then review each definition.

-The suffix **ness**, when added to a word, means **state of** or **condition of**.

-The suffix **ist**, when added to a word, means **one who**.

-The suffix **ant**, when added to a word, means **one who** or **something that**.

List Words		Definitions
cheapness	*cheapness*	• The condition of not wanting to pay too much for something.
emptiness	*emptiness*	• The condition of not containing anything.
laziness	*laziness*	• The condition of not being willing to work.
happiness	*happiness*	• The condition of feeling joy.
liveliness	*liveliness*	• The condition of being full of life.
opportunist	*opportunist*	• One who takes advantage of a situation to benefit himself.
activist	*activist*	• One who is an active member of a cause.
strategist	*strategist*	• One who forms a plan to accomplish a task.
receptionist	*receptionist*	• One who receives or greets visitors to an office.
resistant	*resistant*	• Something that resists or fights against something else.
consultant	*consultant*	• Someone who consults or advises.
buoyant	*buoyant*	• Something that can float in water or in the air.
resultant	*resultant*	• Something that comes from something else.
attendant	*attendant*	• One who is present at a function or job.

2. **Take Your Pretest**
Turn to the next page to the Pretest section and your teacher will ask you to write each list word one at a time.

Pretest - Lesson 23:   Correction Area:

1. _____   _____

2. _____   _____

3. _____   _____

4. _____   _____

5. _____   _____

6. _____   _____

7. _____   _____

8. _____   _____

9. _____   _____

10. _____   _____

11. _____   _____

12. _____   _____

13. _____   _____

14. _____   _____

Carry-over Words: Correction Area:

1. _____   _____

2. _____   _____

3. _____   _____

4. _____   _____

Lesson 23
Day 2

cheapness	happiness	strategist	buoyant
emptiness	liveliness	receptionist	resultant
laziness	opportunist	resistant	attendant
	activist	consultant	

A. Find and circle each list word in the puzzle below.

U N P Z R T B U O Y A N T W S
U H A P P I N E S S Z G C S S
R U M M N O P A R L R C E O E
Q E X T S P D Z T E H L M J N
S O C S J P L W S L I N P A P
S M W E H O T U P V U J T Q A
E D U W P R L S E F I S I W E
N Y M K J T E L I S N L N X H
I E Y X A U I S H V W S E O C
Z L R N Y N W O I Y I K S K C
A A T C E I N Q N S P T S V F
L E P S J S V P R I T K C Q B
A F S N O T G Q F V S A T A T
T S I G E T A R T S N T N G S
C T N A D N E T T A W I N T B

B. Copy the following sentence. **The receptionist welcomed the activist who was hired to work as a consultant.**

_____

_____

_____

_____

**Lesson 23
Day 3**

cheapness	happiness	strategist	buoyant
emptiness	liveliness	receptionist	resultant
laziness	opportunist	resistant	attendant
	activist	consultant	

A. Underline the list words in each sentence.

1. The emptiness of the room was apparent after moving out.

2. His son's laziness was disappointing to Jim.

3. His resultant cold was from an infection.

4. Dan was an attendant at the boat show.

5. Erin was an opportunist while hunting for a job.

6. Cathy was a receptionist for a large company in town.

7. The boat cushion was buoyant in the lake.

8. Because of her cheapness, she would not order two deserts.

9. Gary was an activist for reducing pollution.

10. The virus was somewhat resistant to the new drug.

11. Her happiness over receiving a promotion was nice to see.

12. The consultant gave us advice about our business.

13. The liveliness of the puppy was fun to watch.

14. Barb was the strategist who arranged the surprise party.

B. Write the definition from Day 1 for the list word **opportunist**.

_____

_____

_____

_____

**Lesson 23
Day 4**

cheapness	happiness	strategist	buoyant
emptiness	liveliness	receptionist	resultant
laziness	opportunist	resistant	attendant
	activist	consultant	

A. Write a list word that matches each definition.

1. One who greets visitors.

   _____

2. Condition of feeling joy.

   _____

3. Not willing to work.

   _____

4. One who is present at a function.

   _____

5. Full of life.

   _____

6. Something that resists something.

   _____

7. Not containing anything.

   _____

8. An active member of a cause.

   _____

9. One who takes advantage.

   _____

10. Someone who advises.

    _____

11. One who forms a plan.

    _____

12. Not wanting to pay much.

    _____

13. Something that can float.

    _____

14. Something that comes from
    something else.

    _____

B. Write the definition from Day 1 for the list word **consultant**.

_____

_____

_____

Lesson 23 - Day 5, Final Test   Correction Area:

1. _____   _____

2. _____   _____

3. _____   _____

4. _____   _____

5. _____   _____

6. _____   _____

7. _____   _____

8. _____   _____

9. _____   _____

10. _____   _____

11. _____   _____

12. _____   _____

13. _____   _____

14. _____   _____

Carry-over Words: Correction Area:

1. _____   _____

2. _____   _____

3. _____   _____

4. _____   _____

**Lesson 24
Review
Day 1**

Review of words that end with
ed, er, and ing

List Words

fulfilled	scattered	bartering	commander
abandoned	laborer	fastening	messenger
confessed	dreaming	wandering	lighter
	protecting	launcher	

A. Finish each list word.

1. f_____

2. _____eni_____

3. d_____

4. w_____

5. ab_____

6. c_____r

7. l_____r

8. la_____

9. sc_____

10. p_____

11. c_____d

12. ___ar_____

13. _____es_____

14. _____gh_____

B. Copy the following sentence. **The laborer confessed to the messenger that he was dreaming of an abandoned launcher that scattered balloons in the air.**

_____

_____

_____

_____

Date: _____

Review of more words that end with **ed**, **er**, and **ing**

List Words

duplicated	manager	involved	updating
educated	consumer	explorer	simulating
lecturer	advertiser	believer	igniting
	concluded	validating	

A. Underline the list words you see in each sentence. Write the list words below in the order they appear.

The explorer was involved in igniting a fire that was used in a ceremony, which concluded the campout event.

1. _____   2. _____

3. _____   4. _____

The advertiser wanted to lure the educated consumer in order to sell them his product for updating software.

5. _____   6. _____

7. _____   8. _____

The lecturer gave his speech to the manager that was duplicated from the one he gave last week.

9. _____   10. _____

11. _____

As a believer of using computers to make money, he was testing and validating his new software that is directed toward simulating profits from investments.

12. _____   13. _____

14. _____

Review of words with the **sh** sound using **sh**, **ci**, **ti**, and **si**

List Words

shoes	conclusion	initial	musician
electrician	official	vacation	spacious
fiction	patient	mission	sharp
	confusion	session	

A. Write a list word to match each definition below.

1. Coverings for the feet.

_____

2. One who has authority.

_____

3. The first or the beginning.

_____

4. A person who works with electricity.

_____

5. A thin, fine edge for cutting.

_____

6. A holiday.

_____

7. Large and roomy.

_____

8. Something that is not fact.

_____

9. Showing calm or tolerance.

_____

10. A task to be accomplished.

_____

11. One who performs music.

_____

12. To be unclear or uncertain.

_____

13. An ending or final decision.

_____

14. A series of meetings.

_____

B. Write the definition from Day 1 for the list word **confusion**.

_____

_____

Lesson 24 Review Day 4

Review of words with suffixes
ful, ment, and less

List Words

improvement	investment	rightful	motionless
appointment	bashful	grateful	reckless
government	beautiful	cordless	tasteless
	watchful	fruitless	

A. Write a list word to complete each sentence. Use each list word only once.

1. Receiving an **A** on this test was an _____ over the last.

2. The steak was not very good; it was burnt and _____.

3. The _____ raised everyone's taxes.

4. The shy baby was _____ and looked away.

5. The colorful flowers looked _____.

6. Sharon was _____ that Aaron helped with the dishes.

7. The security guard was _____ over the warehouse.

8. The snake sat _____ as it waited to strike.

9. Katie accepted the _____ as a public official.

10. Patty made an _____ in stocks and bonds.

11. Marge took the _____ telephone outside to speak.

12. Although Darren worked hard, his efforts were _____.

13. Lisa's actions were _____ and caused damage.

14. James was the _____ owner of the radio.

B. Write the definition from Day 1 for the list word **appointment**.

_____

_____

_____

Date: _____

Review of words with suffixes **ness**, **ist**, and **ant**

List Words

cheapness	happiness	strategist	buoyant
emptiness	liveliness	receptionist	resultant
laziness	opportunist	resistant	attendant
	activist	consultant	

A. Draw a line to connect each list word with its definition.

cheapness	One who is present at a function or job.
happiness	It comes from something else.
activist	Can float in water.
resistant	Consults or advises.
emptiness	Resists or fights against something else.
liveliness	Receives or greets visitors in an office.
strategist	Forms a plan to accomplish a task.
consultant	An active member of a cause.
laziness	Takes advantage of a situation.
opportunist	Full of life.
receptionist	Feeling joy.
buoyant	Not being willing to work.
resultant	Not containing anything.
attendant	Not wanting to pay much for something.

B. Underline the list words you see in the following sentence.

The receptionist was a good strategist as well as an opportunist.

Her liveliness and happiness overcame everyone else's laziness, and

the task was finally accomplished.

<<Intentionally left blank>>

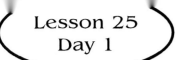

Lesson 25
Day 1

Date: _____

Words that mean **empty**

1. **Review Your List Words**
   Look at the list words below and read each word to yourself. Then review each definition.

   Each of the words below has the same or similar meaning to the word **empty**.

List Words		Definitions
vacant	*vacant*	• Not used or lived in.
void	*void*	• Containing no matter. Also, not valid.
unoccupied	*unoccupied*	• Not being used.
bare	*bare*	• Having no covering.
hollow	*hollow*	• A cavity, gap, or space.
blank	*blank*	• An empty space to be filled in.
clear	*clear*	• Easy to see through.
devoid	*devoid*	• Something that is entirely lacking.
vacuous	*vacuous*	• Devoid of matter. Also, lacking intelligence.
drained	*drained*	• Caused liquid to go out from.
unfilled	*unfilled*	• Not been made full.
barren	*barren*	• Lacking useful vegetation.
cavity	*cavity*	• A hollow. A hole.
abandoned	*abandoned*	• Deserted.

2. **Take Your Pretest**
   Turn to the next page to the Pretest section and your teacher will ask you to write each list word one at a time.

Level 5, Lesson 25 –Words that mean **empty**

145

Pretest - Lesson 25:   Correction Area:

1.   _____   _____

2.   _____   _____

3.   _____   _____

4.   _____   _____

5.   _____   _____

6.   _____   _____

7.   _____   _____

8.   _____   _____

9.   _____   _____

10.   _____   _____

11.   _____   _____

12.   _____   _____

13.   _____   _____

14.   _____   _____

Carry-over Words: Correction Area:

1.   _____   _____

2.   _____   _____

3.   _____   _____

4.   _____   _____

**Lesson 25
Day 2**

Date: _____

vacant	bare	devoid	barren
void	hollow	vacuous	cavity
unoccupied	blank	drained	abandoned
	clear	unfilled	

A. Use the following code to finish the sentences.

A	B	C	D	E	F	G	H	I	J	K	L	M	N	O	P	Q	R	S	T	U	V	W	X	Y	Z
Ω	☺	⌂	✾	☞	☺	✳	☼	✐	✎	◈	◆	✿	⌘	❖	✈	◆	☉	◷	✪	✢	✖	⧗	ᴖ	☎	▥

1. The hotel room was __ __ __ __ __ __ __ __ __ __ during the weekend.

2. Max had to __ __ __ __ the erroneous bill to his customer.

3. The old lawn mower had been __ __ __ __ __ __ __ __ __ .
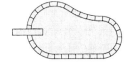

4. The desert was a vast __ __ __ __ __ __ land.

5. David had a __ __ __ __ __ __ in one of his front teeth.

6. The animal had a __ __ __ __ __ __ __ expression.

7. The apartment was __ __ __ __ __ __ after Brad moved out.

8. It took a long time to __ __ __ __ __ __ out the wood to make a bowl.

9. The peeled apple was __ __ __ __ .

10. Mom __ __ __ __ __ __ __ the water from the pool.

11. The new piece of paper was __ __ __ __ __ .

12. Many of the orders for new cars remained __ __ __ __ __ __ __ __ .

13. The window was just cleaned, so it was __ __ __ __ __ .

14. The training was __ __ __ __ __ __ of any real education.

Lesson 25
Day 3

vacant	bare	devoid	barren
void	hollow	vacuous	cavity
unoccupied	blank	drained	abandoned
	clear	unfilled	

A. Write each group of three list words in alphabetical order.

void, vacant, vacuous

1. _____ 2. _____ 3. _____

drained, unfilled, unoccupied

4. _____ 5. _____ 6. _____

clear, cavity, bare

7. _____ 8. _____ 9. _____

devoid, abandoned, blank

10. _____ 11. _____ 12. _____

blank, barren, bare

13. _____ 14. _____ 15. _____

hollow, unoccupied, void

16. _____ 17. _____ 18. _____

devoid, blank, unfilled

19. _____ 20. _____ 21. _____

vacuous, bare, abandoned

22. _____ 23. _____ 24. _____

void, barren, hollow

25. _____ 26. _____ 27. _____

**Lesson 25
Day 4**

vacant	bare	devoid	barren
void	hollow	vacuous	cavity
unoccupied	blank	drained	abandoned
	clear	unfilled	

A. Unscramble the following list words.

vcaatn

1._____

abadndeon

2._____

brrena

3._____

cvatiy

4._____

unccueodpi

5._____

bnkla

6._____

uniedllf

7._____

dredain

8._____

earb

9._____

vdoi

10._____

crlae

11._____

dveodi

12._____

hoowll

13._____

vaucous

14._____

B. Copy the following sentence. **The apartment of the college students was abandoned and had been vacant and unoccupied for quite some time.**

_____

_____

_____

_____

Lesson 25 - Day 5, Final Test

Correction Area:

1. _____ _____

2. _____ _____

3. _____ _____

4. _____ _____

5. _____ _____

6. _____ _____

7. _____ _____

8. _____ _____

9. _____ _____

10. _____ _____

11. _____ _____

12. _____ _____

13. _____ _____

14. _____ _____

Carry-over Words: Correction Area:

1. _____ _____

2. _____ _____

3. _____ _____

4. _____ _____

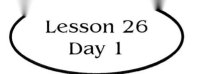

Date: _____

Present and past tense words

1. Review Your List Words

Look at the list words below and read each word to yourself. Then review each definition.

The **present** and **past tense** of each word are listed below.

List Words		Definitions
fight	*fight*	• A struggle or combat. Present tense.
fought	*fought*	• The past tense of fight.
shoot	*shoot*	• To throw something with force. Present tense.
shot	*shot*	• The past tense of shoot.
think	*think*	• To use the mind's power to make decisions. Present tense.
thought	*thought*	• The past tense of think.
stand	*stand*	• To stay in an upright position on the feet. Present tense.
stood	*stood*	• The past tense of stand.
spend	*spend*	• To pay out money or use something. Present tense.
spent	*spent*	• The past tense of spend.
catch	*catch*	• To take hold of or capture something. Present tense.
caught	*caught*	• The past tense of catch.
sleep	*sleep*	• A period of unconscious rest. Present tense.
slept	*slept*	• The past tense of sleep.

2. Take Your Pretest

Turn to the next page to the Pretest section and your teacher will ask you to write each list word one at a time.

Date: _____

Pretest - Lesson 26:   Correction Area:

1. _____   _____

2. _____   _____

3. _____   _____

4. _____   _____

5. _____   _____

6. _____   _____

7. _____   _____

8. _____   _____

9. _____   _____

10. _____   _____

11. _____   _____

12. _____   _____

13. _____   _____

14. _____   _____

Carry-over Words: Correction Area:

1. _____   _____

2. _____   _____

3. _____   _____

4. _____   _____

Level 5, Lesson 26 –**Present** and **past tense** words   152

Lesson 26 Day 2

Date: _____

fight	shot	stood	caught
fought	think	spend	sleep
shoot	thought	spent	slept
	stand	catch	

A. Finish the crossword puzzle.

Across:
1. Upright on your feet. (present)
2. Past tense of sleep.
3. To throw with force. (present)
5. To pay out. (present)
6. Struggle or combat. (present)
8. To capture something. (present)
9. To use the mind to make decisions. (present)

Down:
1. A period of rest. (present)
2. Past tense of stand.
3. Past tense of spend.
4. Past tense of think.
6. Past tense of fight.
7. Past tense of shoot.
8. Past tense of catch

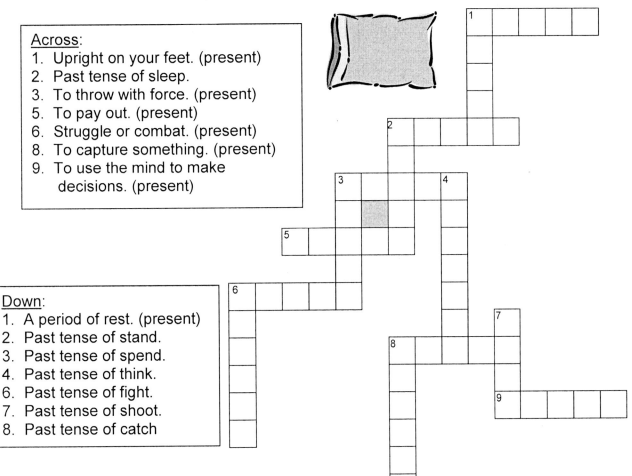

B. Copy the following sentence. **The baseball player could stand still until it was time to catch the shot thrown to her.**

_____

_____

_____

_____

**Lesson 26
Day 3**

fight	shot	stood	caught
fought	think	spend	sleep
shoot	thought	spent	slept
	stand	catch	

A. Draw a line to connect the matching pairs of **present** and **past tense** list words.

fight	slept
sleep	spend
shoot	thought
spent	stood
catch	shot
think	caught
stand	fought

B. Read the following paragraphs and write on the lines below the list words you see. Notice the similarity of the paragraphs?

After getting some sleep, he thought he should get a chance to shoot and catch the basketball. He was in for a real fight as he spent the next thirty minutes trying to make a basket while he stood at the half-court line.

1. _____   2. _____

3. _____   4. _____

5. _____   6. _____

7. _____

After he slept, it was time to think about getting a shot at scoring some baskets with the basketball he caught. He fought hard and would spend the next thirty minutes trying to make a basket. He had to stand at the half-court line.

8. _____   9. _____

10. _____   11. _____

12. _____   13. _____

14. _____

**Lesson 26
Day 4**

fight	shot	stood	caught
fought	think	spend	sleep
shoot	thought	spent	slept
	stand	catch	

A. Write the list word that completes each sentence.

1. Alfred would _____ too much money for the shirt.

2. He would _____ the basketball towards the basket.

3. The team _____ a hard battle and won the game.

4. Terry will _____ for the boxing title.

5. Barry _____ the baseball as it flew towards him.

6. Bruce _____ all of the money his mother gave him.

7. Wilma _____ the basketball into the basket.

8. My brother will go to _____ after a bedtime story.

9. Brook _____ that her homework was completed.

10. You should _____ before you say something hurtful.

11. Mary _____ all day after staying up too late.

12. Darren _____ upright in front of the audience.

13. Claire will _____ the ball if it flies near her.

14. After her leg healed, Donna was able to finally _____ again.

B. Write the definition from Day 1 for the list word **sleep**.

_____

_____

C. Write the definition from Day 1 for the list word **stand**.

_____

_____

Lesson 26 - Day 5, Final Test   Correction Area:

1. _____   _____

2. _____   _____

3. _____   _____

4. _____   _____

5. _____   _____

6. _____   _____

7. _____   _____

8. _____   _____

9. _____   _____

10. _____   _____

11. _____   _____

12. _____   _____

13. _____   _____

14. _____   _____

Carry-over Words: Correction Area:

1. _____   _____

2. _____   _____

3. _____   _____

4. _____   _____

**Lesson 27
Day 1**

Adding **ed**, **er**, **ly**, and **ing**
to words ending in **y**

1. Review Your List Words

Look at the list words below and read each word to yourself. Then review each definition.

There are a few rules to follow when adding an ending to words that end with **y**.

-When **y** follows a **vowel**, you add **ed** or **ing** without changing the spelling of the base word.   **delay + ing = delaying** and **employ + ed = employed**

-When **y** follows a **consonant**, you change the **y** to **i** and add **ed**, **er**, or **ly**. **marry + ed = married**   **heavy + er = heavier**   **angry + ly = angrily**

-However, when **y** follows a **consonant**, you add **ing** without changing the spelling of the base word. **supply + ing = supplying**

List Words		Definitions
supplying	*supplying*	• The act of providing something.
heavier	*heavier*	• Something that weighs more than another.
steadier	*steadier*	• Something that is more stable than another is.
hurrying	*hurrying*	• The act of moving in a swift manner.
delaying	*delaying*	• The act of waiting or putting something off.
married	*married*	• Having a husband or a wife.
studied	*studied*	• To have spent time gaining knowledge.
employed	*employed*	• To work for pay under an employer. Having a job.
happier	*happier*	• More joyful compared to something else.
carrier	*carrier*	• One who carries or transports something.
angrily	*angrily*	• Doing something in an angry manner.
amplifying	*amplifying*	• The act of increasing the volume of sound.
lazily	*lazily*	• Doing something in a slow or sluggish manner.
busily	*busily*	• Doing something in a busy manner.

2. Take Your Pretest

Turn to the next page to the Pretest section and your teacher will ask you to write each list word one at a time.

Pretest - Lesson 27:   Correction Area:

1. _____   _____

2. _____   _____

3. _____   _____

4. _____   _____

5. _____   _____

6. _____   _____

7. _____   _____

8. _____   _____

9. _____   _____

10. _____   _____

11. _____   _____

12. _____   _____

13. _____   _____

14. _____   _____

Carry-over Words: Correction Area:

1. _____   _____

2. _____   _____

3. _____   _____

4. _____   _____

**Lesson 27
Day 2**

supplying	hurrying	employed	amplifying
heavier	delaying	happier	lazily
steadier	married	carrier	busily
	studied	angrily	

A. Unscramble the following list words.

stieread

1._____

caierrr

2._____

suyppling

3._____

miedarr

4._____

blyusi

5._____

hieeavr

6._____

deinglay

7._____

arilngy

8._____

hierapp

9._____

setudid

10._____

liazly

11._____

aifmplying

12._____

eoympled

13._____

hyiurrng

14._____

B. Copy the following sentence. **The married man was happier when he was employed by a large freight carrier.**

_____

_____

_____

_____

**Lesson 27
Day 3**

supplying	hurrying	employed	amplifying
heavier	delaying	happier	lazily
steadier	married	carrier	busily
	studied	angrily	

A. Find and circle each list word in the puzzle below.

```
L   L   Y   D   R   F   C   N   S   R   O   X   M   D   M
W   Q   L   E   C   B   C   J   Q   I   R   V   E   H   A
O   B   I   I   F   T   E   G   S   E   F   L   A   U   R
H   X   S   D   J   V   A   F   I   A   A   P   K   R   R
R   C   U   U   A   A   T   R   A   Y   P   F   B   R   I
S   E   B   T   A   N   R   N   I   I   X   I   F   Y   E
D   U   I   S   U   A   G   N   E   B   I   F   P   I   D
O   V   P   D   C   O   G   R   C   R   Z   T   P   N   C
H   U   H   P   A   M   P   L   I   F   Y   I   N   G   E
Z   X   I   B   L   E   J   V   R   L   X   Q   D   S   F
O   V   K   Y   D   Y   T   H   S   E   Y   M   L   Y   P
Y   L   I   Z   A   L   I   S   H   E   A   V   I   E   R
C   C   U   Z   I   N   J   N   W   A   N   L   S   M   J
D   Z   U   K   R   W   A   L   G   M   V   E   X   N   V
D   E   Y   O   L   P   M   E   B   T   V   N   K   A   M
```

B. Write the definition from Day 1 for the list word **hurrying**.

_____

_____

C. Write the definition from Day 1 for the list word **carrier**.

_____

_____

**Lesson 27
Day 4**

supplying	hurrying	employed	amplifying
heavier	delaying	happier	lazily
steadier	married	carrier	busily
	studied	angrily	

A. Draw a line to connect each list word with its definition.

busily   Doing something in a busy manner.

happier   Doing something in a sluggish manner.

employed   The act of increasing the volume of sound.

steadier   Doing something in an angry manner.

heavier   One who carries or transports something.

supplying   More joyful compared to something else.

amplifying   To work for pay under an employer.

angrily   To have spent time gaining knowledge.

carrier   Having a husband or a wife.

lazily   The act of waiting or putting something off.

married   The act of moving in a swift manner.

delaying   Something that is more stable than another.

hurrying   Something that weighs more than another.

studied   The act of providing something.

B. Cross out the word that is spelled incorrectly.

1. (carryer, carrier)
2. (maried, married)
3. (hurrying, hurring)
4. (studyed, studied)
5. (heavier, hevvier)
6. (steadier, stediar)
7. (busily, buisily)

8. (laziley, lazily)
9. (delaying, delaiying)
10. (agriley, angrily)
11. (amplifying, amplefying)
12. (suplying, supplying)
13. (employed, emploid)
14. (happyier, happier)

Lesson 27 - Day 5, Final Test   Correction Area:

1.   _____   _____

2.   _____   _____

3.   _____   _____

4.   _____   _____

5.   _____   _____

6.   _____   _____

7.   _____   _____

8.   _____   _____

9.   _____   _____

10. _____   _____

11. _____   _____

12. _____   _____

13. _____   _____

14. _____   _____

Carry-over Words: Correction Area:

1.   _____   _____

2.   _____   _____

3.   _____   _____

4.   _____   _____

**Lesson 28
Day 1**

Words with consonant digraphs
wh, **ch**, **tch**, **sh**, and **th**

1. **Review Your List Words**
Look at the list words below and read each word to yourself. Then review each definition.

A consonant **digraph** is two or three consonants that act together to make one sound.

List Words		Definitions
bu<u>tch</u>er	*butcher*	• Someone who cuts, packages, and sells meat.
dispa<u>tch</u>	*dispatch*	• To send away quickly with a message.
splo<u>tch</u>	*splotch*	• An irregularly shaped spot or stain.
<u>wh</u>imper	*whimper*	• A low-toned, hesitant cry.
<u>wh</u>isper	*whisper*	• A very soft manner of speaking.
else<u>wh</u>ere	*elsewhere*	• In some other place.
<u>ch</u>eerful	*cheerful*	• To be happy or pleasant.
ar<u>ch</u>ive	*archive*	• A place where important papers are stored.
ex<u>ch</u>ange	*exchange*	• To trade something for something else.
mar<u>sh</u>al	*marshal*	• One who directs an event such as a parade.
member<u>sh</u>ip	*membership*	• Being a part of a club or organization.
ca<u>sh</u>ew	*cashew*	• A kidney-shaped, edible nut from a tree.
lea<u>th</u>er	*leather*	• Tanned and prepared animal hide.
ma<u>th</u>ematics	*mathematics*	• The science of studying numbers, measurements, and quantities.

2. **Take Your Pretest**
Turn to the next page to the Pretest section and your teacher will ask you to write each list word one at a time.

Pretest – Lesson 28:   Correction Area:

1. _____   _____

2. _____   _____

3. _____   _____

4. _____   _____

5. _____   _____

6. _____   _____

7. _____   _____

8. _____   _____

9. _____   _____

10. _____   _____

11. _____   _____

12. _____   _____

13. _____   _____

14. _____   _____

Carry-over Words: Correction Area:

1. _____   _____

2. _____   _____

3. _____   _____

4. _____   _____

**Lesson 28
Day 2**

butcher	whimper	archive	cashew
dispatch	whisper	exchange	leather
splotch	elsewhere	marshal	mathematics
	cheerful	membership	

A. Read each clue. Write a list word in the blanks that answers each clue.
   Read down the shaded cells to find the answer to the question asked.
   Write the answer to the question in the spaces provided.

1. He cuts and sells meat.

2. A soft voice.

3. An irregular spot.

4. Tanned animal hide.

5. A place for storage.

6. Part of an organization.

7. A kidney-shaped nut.

8. Send with a message.

   "Why could the bicycle not stand up on its own?"

   Answer: It was ____ ____ ____   ____ ____ ____ ____ ____.

B. Write the definition from Day 1 for the list word **mathematics**.

   _____

   _____

   _____

   _____

C. Write the definition from Day 1 for the list word **archive**.

   _____

   _____

   _____

**Lesson 28
Day 3**

butcher	whimper	archive	cashew
dispatch	whisper	exchange	leather
splotch	elsewhere	marshal	mathematics
	cheerful	membership	

A. Write each group of three list words in alphabetical order.

cheerful, cashew, butcher

1. _____   2. _____   3. _____

whimper, marshal, whisper

4. _____   5. _____   6. _____

elsewhere, exchange, dispatch

7. _____   8. _____   9. _____

exchange, mathematics, leather

10. _____   11. _____ 12. _____

membership, marshal, mathematics

13. _____   14. _____ 15. _____

splotch, whimper, cashew

16. _____   17. _____ 18. _____

exchange, archive , leather

19. _____   20. _____ 21. _____

marshal, whisper, cheerful

22. _____   23. _____ 24. _____

butcher, leather, cashew

25. _____   26. _____ 27. _____

**9
x 1**

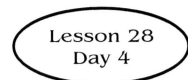

**Lesson 28
Day 4**

butcher	whimper	archive	cashew
dispatch	whisper	exchange	leather
splotch	elsewhere	marshal	mathematics
	cheerful	membership	

A. Finish each list word.

1. b_____

2. el_____

3. d_____

4. __eat_____

5. mat_____

6. ___she_____

7. __p_____

8. _____isp_____

9. a_____

10. __x_____

11. ___im_____

12. ch_____

13. _____al

14. _____ip

B. Copy the following sentence. **Matthew wanted to exchange his leather coat for a new one because it had a splotch of ketchup on it.**

_____

_____

_____

_____

_____

C. Write the definition from Day 1 for the list word **cheerful**.

_____

_____

Date: _____

Lesson 28 - Day 5, Final Test   <u>Correction Area</u>:

1. _____   _____

2. _____   _____

3. _____   _____

4. _____   _____

5. _____   _____

6. _____   _____

7. _____   _____

8. _____   _____

9. _____   _____

10. _____   _____

11. _____   _____

12. _____   _____

13. _____   _____

14. _____   _____

<u>Carry-over Words</u>:   <u>Correction Area</u>:

1. _____   _____

2. _____   _____

3. _____   _____

4. _____   _____

Date: _____

Words with **ll**, **tt**, **ss**, **zz**, and **ff**

1. **Review Your List Words**
   Look at the list words below and read each word to yourself. Then review each definition.

cattle	*cattle*	• Animals that have hooves and are raised for their meat and leather.
battle	*battle*	• A fight between people or animals.
brittle	*brittle*	• Very hard but easily broken.
alleged	*alleged*	• To make an accusation without proof.
address	*address*	• The description of the location where a person lives or works as written on mail.
chilly	*chilly*	• A bit cold.
collide	*collide*	• To come together with direct impact.
aggressive	*aggressive*	• Behaving in a hostile fashion.
blizzard	*blizzard*	• A snowstorm that is heavy.
buzzer	*buzzer*	• An electrical device that emits a warning sound.
distress	*distress*	• Anxiety or mental suffering.
affection	*affection*	• A feeling of fondness for someone or something.
affordable	*affordable*	• An amount that can be easily paid.
shuffle	*shuffle*	• To jumble or mix something up.

2. **Take Your Pretest**
   Turn to the next page to the Pretest section and your teacher will ask you to write each list word one at a time.

Pretest - Lesson 29:   Correction Area:

1. _____   _____

2. _____   _____

3. _____   _____

4. _____   _____

5. _____   _____

6. _____   _____

7. _____   _____

8. _____   _____

9. _____   _____

10. _____   _____

11. _____   _____

12. _____   _____

13. _____   _____

14. _____   _____

Carry-over Words: Correction Area:

1. _____   _____

2. _____   _____

3. _____   _____

4. _____   _____

**Lesson 29
Day 2**

cattle	alleged	aggressive	affection
battle	address	blizzard	affordable
brittle	chilly	buzzer	shuffle
	collide	distress	

A. Write the list word that completes each sentence.

1. The _____ stood in the field as a herd.

2. The shirt was _____ because it was on sale.

3. He had to _____ the cards before playing the game.

4. Tamy had a great _____ for good Mexican food.

5. The hard candy was tasty but very _____.

6. It was very _____ in Alaska during the winter.

7. The _____ of the office was 100 Main Street.

8. The _____ made it hard to travel through the snow.

9. The two airplanes will _____ if they are not careful.

10. It was _____ that Jacob took the last cookie.

11. The bear was very _____ and scared the campers.

12. Todd felt some _____ after eating the spoiled food.

13. Diane pressed the _____ to alert them of her arrival.

14. The armies prepared to do _____ in the empty field.

B. Write the definition from Day 1 for the list word **battle**.

_____

_____

C. Write the definition from Day 1 for the list word **alleged**.

_____

_____

Date: _____

cattle	alleged	aggressive	affection
battle	address	blizzard	affordable
brittle	chilly	buzzer	shuffle
	collide	distress	

A. Finish the crossword puzzle.

Across:
3. Hard but easily broken.
7. Description of a location as written on mail.
9. A bit cold.
11. Behaving in a hostile fashion.
12. To accuse without proof.

Down:
1. To mix up.
2. To come together with direct impact.
3. An electrical warning device.
4. Anxiety.
5. A feeling of fondness.
6. Hoofed animals in a herd.
8. To fight.
10. Heavy snowstorm.
11. Easy to purchase.

**Lesson 29
Day 4**

cattle	alleged	aggressive	affection
battle	address	blizzard	affordable
brittle	chilly	buzzer	shuffle
	collide	distress	

A. Unscramble the following list words.

suhffel

1._____

afodfrlabe

2._____

bttreli

3. _____

bzizldra

4._____

cilolde

5. _____

bzezru

6._____

ctatel

7. _____

aleldeg

8._____

adresds

9. _____

cilhly

10._____

btteal

11. _____

dstrssei

12._____

agessrgeiv

13. _____

afecfotin

14._____

B. Copy the following sentence. **The cattle were in distress because they were standing in a chilly blizzard all day.**

_____

_____

_____

_____

Lesson 29 - Day 5, Final Test

Correction Area:

1. _____   _____

2. _____   _____

3. _____   _____

4. _____   _____

5. _____   _____

6. _____   _____

7. _____   _____

8. _____   _____

9. _____   _____

10. _____   _____

11. _____   _____

12. _____   _____

13. _____   _____

14. _____   _____

Carry-over Words: Correction Area:

1. _____   _____

2. _____   _____

3. _____   _____

4. _____   _____

**Lesson 30
Review
Day 1**

Review of words that mean **empty**

List Words

vacant	bare	devoid	barren
void	hollow	vacuous	cavity
unoccupied	blank	drained	abandoned
	clear	unfilled	

A. Find and circle each list word in the puzzle below.

```
P  A  N  B  D  B  V  Y  B  F  C  Y  O  D  B

G  O  E  L  E  I  P  A  F  Z  T  U  E  D  A

I  R  R  W  I  V  O  X  C  I  H  N  G  Z  R

B  J  R  J  P  A  P  V  V  U  O  I  J  I  E

G  F  A  M  U  C  Y  A  E  D  O  Q  Q  S  X

A  B  B  V  C  A  C  G  N  D  D  U  Y  I  I

P  A  L  H  C  N  E  A  C  E  E  I  S  J  T

L  E  D  A  O  T  B  U  N  F  I  L  L  E  D

T  S  Q  C  N  A  D  I  C  L  E  A  R  D  F

G  D  U  I  U  K  A  W  O  L  L  O  H  V  B

V  S  R  U  O  R  X  D  J  Y  Q  U  O  G  Y

Z  C  Q  H  D  T  L  W  E  O  W  I  G  B  A

G  X  W  N  J  B  I  W  M  J  D  P  N  E  T

J  U  G  H  Q  L  C  M  J  R  D  M  E  Z  P

E  X  O  Q  V  C  A  L  I  F  Z  U  U  J  H
```

Date: _____

Review of **present** and **past** tense words

List Words

fight	shot	stood	caught
fought	think	spend	sleep
shoot	thought	spent	slept
	stand	catch	

A. Read each clue. Write a list word in the blanks that answers each clue. Read down the shaded cells to find the answer to the question asked. Write the answer to the question in the spaces provided.

1. Past tense of shoot.

2. A period of rest. (present)

3. Past tense of spend.

4. Upright on one's feet. (present)

5. Your mind at work. (present)

6. Past tense of sleep.

7. To pay out money. (present)

8. Past tense of stand.

9. Combat. (present)

10. To capture something. (present)

"The builder did a good job constructing the house. You could say…"

Answer: ____ ____ ____ ____ ____ ____ ____ ____ ____ ____!

B. Write the definition from Day 1 for the list word **think**.

_____

_____

**Lesson 30
Review
Day 3**

Review of adding **ed**, **er**, **ly**, and **ing** to words ending in **y**

List Words

supplying	hurrying	employed	amplifying
heavier	delaying	happier	lazily
steadier	married	carrier	busily
	studied	angrily	

A. Write a list word to complete each sentence. Use each list word only once.

1. Toby was _____ to catch the bus.

2. He was _____ the time when he had to do homework.

3. The couple was _____ in June.

4. _____ the sound ensured that everyone would hear it.

5. She was _____ on her feet than her taller brother.

6. The boulder was _____ than the small rock.

7. Frances was _____ as a clerk at the local post office.

8. The _____ delivered the package to us last week.

9. The caged raccoon _____ bit at his captors.

10. They _____ rested on the sunny afternoon.

11. Luke _____ all night for his test in biology.

12. Brooke was _____ than her brother who got into trouble.

13. Mia _____ went about the process of planning the party.

14. Greg's business is _____ fresh fish to the local restaurant.

B. Write the definition from Day 1 for the list word **heavier**.

_____

_____

Date: _____

Review of words with consonant digraphs **wh**, **ch**, **tch**, **sh**, and **th**

List Words

butcher	whimper	archive	cashew
dispatch	whisper	exchange	leather
splotch	elsewhere	marshal	mathematics
	cheerful	membership	

A. Unscramble the following list words.

mtheamtaics

1._____

cshwea

2._____

laereth

3._____

eselhewre

4._____

dpsaitch

5._____

sthoplc

6._____

wihpers

7._____

cehreluf

8._____

mrahsla

9._____

wimhepr

10._____

mmberepihs

11._____

acrhvie

12._____

bthucre

13._____

ehcxgena

14._____

**Lesson 30
Review
Day 5**

Review of words with
ll, tt, ss, zz, and ff

List Words

cattle	alleged	aggressive	affection
battle	address	blizzard	affordable
brittle	chilly	buzzer	shuffle
	collide	distress	

A. Write each group of three list words in alphabetical order.

chilly, collide, cattle

1. _____   2. _____   3. _____

shuffle, distress, buzzer

4. _____   5. _____   6. _____

brittle, battle, blizzard

7. _____   8. _____   9. _____

buzzer, distress, cattle

10. _____   11. _____   12. _____

address, aggressive, affordable

13. _____   14. _____   15. _____

alleged, affection, address

16. _____   17. _____   18. _____

collide, battle, aggressive

19. _____   20. _____   21. _____

affordable, affection, alleged

22. _____   23. _____   24. _____

<<Intentionally left blank>>

Lesson 31
Day 1

Words with vowel blends
o**i**, o**y**, o**u**, and o**w**

1. **Review Your List Words**
   Look at the list words below and read each word to yourself. Then review each definition.

   The letters **oi** and **oy** can make the sound **oi** as in **oil**. Examples: ch**oi**ce and ann**oy**

   The letters **ow** can make the **ow** sound as in **cow** or the long **o** sound as in **no**. Examples: all**ow**ed and overfl**ow**

   The letters **ou** can make the short **u** sound as in **bus**, the **oo** sound as in **too**, or the **ow** sound as in **cow**. Examples : d**ou**ble, t**ou**r, and ast**ou**nd

List Words		Definitions
ch**oi**ce	*choice*	• Choosing from more than one.
her**oi**c	*heroic*	• Being courageous or fearless.
m**oi**sten	*moisten*	• To make slightly wet.
ann**oy**	*annoy*	• To irritate or bother.
destr**oy**	*destroy*	• To do away with or damage.
v**oy**age	*voyage*	• A long journey by water.
d**ou**ble	*double*	• Twice the number of something else.
t**ou**r	*tour*	• Traveling for pleasure.
overfl**ow**	*overflow*	• To flow out of the top of something.
ast**ou**nd	*astound*	• Confusion that amazes.
all**ow**ed	*allowed*	• To permit or to allow to happen.
borr**ow**	*borrow*	• To take something for use with the promise of returning it.
outgr**ow**n	*outgrown*	• To become too large for something.
t**ow**ard	*toward*	• In the direction of.

2. **Take Your Pretest**
   Turn to the next page to the Pretest section and your teacher will ask you to write each list word one at a time.

Date: _____

Correction Area:

1. _____ _____

2. _____ _____

3. _____ _____

4. _____ _____

5. _____ _____

6. _____ _____

7. _____ _____

8. _____ _____

9. _____ _____

10. _____ _____

11. _____ _____

12. _____ _____

13. _____ _____

14. _____ _____

Carry-over Words: Correction Area:

1. _____ _____

2. _____ _____

3. _____ _____

4. _____ _____

Lesson 31
Day 2

choice	annoy	tour	borrow
heroic	destroy	overflow	outgrown
moisten	voyage	astound	toward
	double	allowed	

A. Finish each list word.

1. h_____

2. _____ar___

3. _____ist_____

4. __ve_____

5. ___nn_____

6. do_____

7. c_____

8. _____tr_____

9. v_____

10. ou__ _____

11. t_____

12. _____ed

13. a___to_____

14. b_____

B. Copy the following sentences. **It was her choice to take either a voyage to Hawaii or a tour of Italy. She was allowed to do both.**

_____

_____

_____

_____

_____

C. Write the definition from Day 1 for the list word **double**.

_____

_____

**Lesson 31
Day 3**

choice	annoy	tour	borrow
heroic	destroy	overflow	outgrown
moisten	voyage	astound	toward
	double	allowed	

A. Read the following sentences and write on the lines below the list words you see.

The voyage would moisten her coat as the overflow of water on the ship's double deck allowed her to get wet.

1. _____   2. _____

3. _____   4. _____

5. _____

His heroic efforts would astound and annoy the villains. It was his choice to send police officers toward the group in an effort to destroy their chances.

6. _____   7. _____

8. _____   9. _____

10. _____   11. _____

Troy and his friends had to borrow money to take a European tour in a rented car. Unfortunately, they soon found that they had outgrown the small car.

12. _____   13. _____

14. _____

B. Write the definition from Day 1 for the list word **overflow**.

_____

_____

Lesson 31
Day 4

choice	annoy	tour	borrow
heroic	destroy	overflow	outgrown
moisten	voyage	astound	toward
	double	allowed	

A. Underline the list word in each group that is spelled correctly.

1. choice   choyce   choicie

2. outgrowne   outgrown   outgroan

3. moissent   mosten   moisten

4. tword   toward   tword

5. borrow   barow   borow

6. heroec   heroic   hearoic

7. anoy   annoye   annoy

8. dubble   double   doubble

9. destroye   destroiye   destroy

10. voyage   voiyage   voyaige

11. ture   tour   toure

12. astound   astownd   astounde

13. allowwed   allowed   aloude

14. overflow   overflowe   oaverflow

B. Copy the following sentences. **The members have outgrown the building and now overflow out onto the street. They need to double their space.**

_____

_____

_____

_____

Lesson 31 - Day 5, Final Test

Correction Area:

1. _____   _____
2. _____   _____
3. _____   _____
4. _____   _____
5. _____   _____
6. _____   _____
7. _____   _____
8. _____   _____
9. _____   _____
10. _____   _____
11. _____   _____
12. _____   _____
13. _____   _____
14. _____   _____

Carry-over Words: Correction Area:

1. _____   _____
2. _____   _____
3. _____   _____
4. _____   _____

Date: _____

Words that mean **fun**

1. Review Your List Words
Look at the list words below and read each word to yourself. Then review each definition.

Each of the words below has something to do with the word **fun**.

List Words		Definitions
excitement	*excitement*	• The state of being agitated or excited.
amusement	*amusement*	• To be entertained by something.
play	*play*	• To be active in an enjoyable manner.
game	*game*	• An activity that has rules where people compete against each other for fun.
joke	*joke*	• To say or do an act with the intention of being funny.
humor	*humor*	• The ability to see the amusing quality of something.
enjoyable	*enjoyable*	• Something that gives one pleasure.
merry	*merry*	• To be full of joy or delight.
comedy	*comedy*	• A funny play or movie.
funny	*funny*	• Something that causes laughter.
entertain	*entertain*	• To do something that captures the interest or amuses people.
frolic	*frolic*	• To be playful.
pleasure	*pleasure*	• A feeling of enjoyment from participating in or viewing an activity.
recreation	*recreation*	• A relaxing or fun time to refresh the mind.

2. Take Your Pretest
Turn to the next page to the Pretest section and your teacher will ask you to write each list word one at a time.

Date: _____

Correction Area:

1. _____   _____

2. _____   _____

3. _____   _____

4. _____   _____

5. _____   _____

6. _____   _____

7. _____   _____

8. _____   _____

9. _____   _____

10. _____   _____

11. _____   _____

12. _____   _____

13. _____   _____

14. _____   _____

Carry-over Words: Correction Area:

1. _____   _____

2. _____   _____

3. _____   _____

4. _____   _____

Lesson 32
Day 2

excitement	game	merry	frolic
amusement	joke	comedy	pleasure
play	humor	funny	recreation
	enjoyable	entertain	

A. Cross out the word that is spelled incorrectly. Write the correctly spelled words on the lines.

1. (excitemant, excitement) _____

2. (gaime, game) _____

3. (play, playe) _____

4. (plesuire, pleasure) _____

5. (frollic, frolic) _____

6. (merrey, merry) _____

7. (funny, funey) _____

8. (enjoyable, enjoyible) _____

9. (entertane, entertain) _____

10. (joke, joak) _____

11. (humer, humor) _____

12. (plentiful, plentful) _____

13. (comdey, comedy) _____

14. (recreation, recraetoin) _____

B. Write the definition from Day 1 for the list word **recreation**.

_____

_____

Lesson 32
Day 3

Date: _____

excitement	game	merry	frolic
amusement	joke	comedy	pleasure
play	humor	funny	recreation
	enjoyable	entertain	

A. Draw a line to connect each list word with its definition. These might be difficult since many are quite similar. Be sure to check your definitions from Day 1.

excitement   An activity that has rules where people compete against each other for fun.

play   A relaxing or fun time to refresh the mind.

amusement   To do something that captures the interest or amuses people.

game   A feeling of enjoyment from participating in or viewing an activity.

humor   Something that gives one pleasure.

joke   To behave playfully.

pleasure   Something that causes laughter.

recreation   To be active in an enjoyable manner.

merry   A funny play or movie.

enjoyable   The ability to see the amusing quality of something.

comedy   To be entertained by something.

funny   To be full of joy or delight.

entertain   Being agitated or excited.

frolic   To say or do an act with the intention of being funny.

B. Write the definition from Day 1 for the list word **merry**.

_____

_____

C. Write the definition from Day 1 for the list word **play**.

_____

_____

Date: _____

excitement	game	merry	frolic
amusement	joke	comedy	pleasure
play	humor	funny	recreation
	enjoyable	entertain	

A. Finish the crossword puzzle. Look at your definitions from Day 1 for help.

Across:
3. To be entertained by something.
7. A funny play or movie.
10. A time to refresh the mind.
12. Something that gives pleasure.
13. To be active in an enjoyable manner.
14. Being agitated or excited.

Down:
1. To say it trying to be funny.
2. An activity that has rules.
4. To be full of joy or delight.
5. To see the amusing quality in something.
6. Feeling of enjoyment from participating in an activity.
8. To be playful.
9. Something that causes laughter.
11. Captures the interest or amuses people.

B. Copy the following sentences. **David saw the humor by the joke that caused excitement at the comedy club. It was funny and enjoyable.**

_____

_____

_____

_____

Lesson 32 - Day 5, Final Test:

Correction Area:

1. _____   _____

2. _____   _____

3. _____   _____

4. _____   _____

5. _____   _____

6. _____   _____

7. _____   _____

8. _____   _____

9. _____   _____

10. _____   _____

11. _____   _____

12. _____   _____

13. _____   _____

14. _____   _____

Carry-over Words:

Correction Area:

1. _____   _____

2. _____   _____

3. _____   _____

4. _____   _____

**Lesson 33
Day 1**

Words with the suffixes
ity and ive

1. Review Your List Words

Look at the list words below and read each word to yourself. Then review each definition.

-The suffix **ity**, when added to a word, means **the state or quality of being**.

-The suffix **ive**, when added to a word, means **tending to** or **having to do with**.

List Words		Definitions
equality	*equality*	• The state of being the same or equal.
originality	*originality*	• The quality of being the same as it originally was when new.
creative	*creative*	• Having to do with making or creating new and original things.
selective	*selective*	• One who is tending to be picky when making a decision.
availability	*availability*	• The state of being obtainable.
density	*density*	• The quality of being dense. The amount or number of something within a given space.
detective	*detective*	• One who has to do with investigating and solving crimes.
electricity	*electricity*	• The quality of having an electric current that makes modern life possible by operating lighting and other useful devices.
superiority	*superiority*	• The state of being better than all others.
supportive	*supportive*	• Having to do with support or assistance.
humidity	*humidity*	• The state of being humid, which is the level of moisture present within the air.
productive	*productive*	• Having to do with producing. Yielding favorable results.
destructive	*destructive*	• Likely to destroy.
objective	*objective*	• Having to do with something worked toward or striven for. A goal.

2. Take Your Pretest

Turn to the next page to the Pretest section and your teacher will ask you to write each list word one at a time.

Date: _____

Correction Area:

1. _____ _____

2. _____ _____

3. _____ _____

4. _____ _____

5. _____ _____

6. _____ _____

7. _____ _____

8. _____ _____

9. _____ _____

10. _____ _____

11. _____ _____

12. _____ _____

13. _____ _____

14. _____ _____

Carry-over Words: Correction Area:

1. _____ _____

2. _____ _____

3. _____ _____

4. _____ _____

Date: _____

equality	selective	electricity	productive
originality	availability	superiority	destructive
creative	density	supportive	objective
	detective	humidity	

A. Use the following code to finish the sentences.

A	B	C	D	E	F	G	H	I	J	K	L	M	N	O	P	Q	R	S	T	U	V	W	X	Y	Z

1. The people demanded _____ for everyone.

2. Shelli was very _____ with her artwork.

3. The crane and wrecking ball can be _____.

4. The _____ of the red batteries was clear.

5. Janet used _____ to run the stove.

6. There was a lot of _____ in the air.

7. They were very _____ with their decision.

8. Betty needed to check Ed's _____.

9. Gail was very _____ of the workers' efforts.

10. Lane liked the old car's _____.

11. The _____ of the foam was perfect for a pillow.

12. The _____ investigated the robbery.

13. Washing windows in the rain was not _____.

14. The _____ of any real education is to learn.

Date: _____

equality	selective	electricity	productive
originality	availability	superiority	destructive
creative	density	supportive	objective
	detective	humidity	

A. **Guide words** are placed at the top of each page of a dictionary to provide an alphabetical guide for finding entry words that appear on that page. For example, assume that a page has the guide words **fast** and **feline**. The entry word **farmer** would not be found on that page because alphabetically it does not fall between these **guide words**. On the other hand, the entry word **feeling** would be found on that page.

Look at each pair of **guide words**. Write the list word on the line that would appear on the dictionary page with those **guide words**.

1. envelope   era   _____

2. elect   elegant   _____

3. dessert   detour   _____

4. process   profit   _____

5. summon   surface   _____

6. seek   sell   _____

7. hug   humor   _____

8. organ   ornate   _____

9. autumn   awake   _____

10. crawl   creek   _____

11. denote   deposit   _____

12. sunset   surround   _____

13. despise   detail   _____

14. obey   obvious   _____

Date: _____

equality	selective	electricity	productive
originality	availability	superiority	destructive
creative	density	supportive	objective
	detective	humidity	

A. Cross out each word that is spelled incorrectly.

1. (equlity, equality)
2. (originated, orignated)
3. (availabilty, availability)
4. (objectuve, objective)
5. (createve, creative)
6. (electcity, electricity)
7. (suppoteve, supportive)

8. (destructive, destructave)
9. (density, densitey)
10. (superiorty, superiority)
11. (productive, productiv)
12. (sellective, selective)
13. (detecteve, detective)
14. (humidity, hummidity)

B. Copy the following sentences. **The detective was very selective in whom he chose to interview. This helped him to be productive and to accomplish his objective.**

_____

_____

_____

_____

C. Write the definition from Day 1 for the list word **equality**.

_____

_____

D. Write the definition from Day 1 for the list word **superiority**.

_____

_____

Lesson 33 - Day 5, Final Test   Correction Area:

1. _____   _____

2. _____   _____

3. _____   _____

4. _____   _____

5. _____   _____

6. _____   _____

7. _____   _____

8. _____   _____

9. _____   _____

10. _____   _____

11. _____   _____

12. _____   _____

13. _____   _____

14. _____   _____

Carry-over Words: Correction Area:

1. _____   _____

2. _____   _____

3. _____   _____

4. _____   _____

**Lesson 34
Day 1**

Words with the suffixes
ence and ance

1. Review Your List Words
Look at the list words below and read each word to yourself. Then review each definition.

-The suffixes **ance** and **ence**, when added to a word, means **the state or quality of being**, **the process of**, or **the act of**.

List Words		Definitions
appearance	*appearance*	• How something looks visually. The process of appearing.
guidance	*guidance*	• Giving direction to someone. The process of giving guidance.
intelligence	*intelligence*	• The ability to learn and make decisions. The quality of being knowledgeable.
enhance	*enhance*	• The process of improving.
entrance	*entrance*	• The act of entering.
reliance	*reliance*	• The act of depending on something or someone.
grievance	*grievance*	• The act of complaining or protesting.
absence	*absence*	• The state of being away or not in attendance.
confidence	*confidence*	• The state or quality of being certain.
experience	*experience*	• The act of participating in something.
patience	*patience*	• The quality of being tolerant.
reference	*reference*	• The act of referring to something.
silence	*silence*	• The quality of being or keeping still.
residence	*residence*	• The act of dwelling in a place. A place where someone lives.

2. Take Your Pretest
Turn to the next page to the Pretest section and your teacher will ask you to write each list word one at a time.

Date: _____

Correction Area:

1. _____   _____

2. _____   _____

3. _____   _____

4. _____   _____

5. _____   _____

6. _____   _____

7. _____   _____

8. _____   _____

9. _____   _____

10. _____   _____

11. _____   _____

12. _____   _____

13. _____   _____

14. _____   _____

Carry-over Words: Correction Area:

1. _____   _____

2. _____   _____

3. _____   _____

4. _____   _____

Date: _____

**Lesson 34
Day 2**

appearance	enhance	absence	reference
guidance	entrance	confidence	silence
intelligence	reliance	experience	residence
	grievance	patience	

A. Find and circle each list word in the puzzle below.

```
I  A  E  D  E  E  H  R  Y  E  Y  E  L  T  E
Y  N  V  C  B  N  E  D  X  I  C  C  L  P  C
E  J  T  G  N  L  T  P  C  N  W  N  Y  A  N
F  C  P  E  I  A  E  R  E  O  Q  E  A  T  E
C  C  N  A  L  R  V  D  A  Y  C  R  P  I  L
A  T  N  E  I  L  I  E  V  N  B  E  P  E  I
L  C  X  E  S  S  I  Q  I  K  C  F  E  N  S
E  O  N  J  E  B  Z  G  D  R  E  E  A  C  J
U  C  S  R  R  F  A  F  E  R  G  R  R  E  J
E  T  E  C  N  E  D  I  F  N  O  C  A  D  K
G  U  I  D  A  N  C  E  U  R  C  V  N  H  U
H  S  X  F  E  C  N  A  H  N  E  E  C  I  S
T  L  K  J  B  S  H  V  T  A  Q  I  E  V  A
Y  S  C  K  U  O  R  I  F  A  K  F  N  M  A
T  F  X  R  E  A  E  V  W  Q  S  L  W  G  G
```

B. Copy the following sentences. **The clean shirt was given to Mike to enhance his appearance and boost his confidence.**

_____

_____

_____

_____

Level 5, Lesson 34 – Words with the suffixes **ence** and **ance**   201

Lesson 34
Day 3

Date: _____

appearance	enhance	absence	reference
guidance	entrance	confidence	silence
intelligence	reliance	experience	residence
	grievance	patience	

A. Write each group of three list words in alphabetical order.

experience, enhance, entrance

1. _____   2. _____   3. _____

appearance, absence, patience

4. _____   5. _____   6. _____

reference, residence, reliance

7. _____   8. _____   9. _____

guidance, intelligence, grievance

10. _____   11. _____   12. _____

patience, intelligence, confidence

13. _____   14. _____   15. _____

silence, residence, reference

16. _____   17. _____   18. _____

enhance, appearance, confidence

19. _____   20. _____   21. _____

grievance, enhance, experience

22. _____   23. _____   24. _____

entrance, confidence, patience

25. _____   26. _____   27. _____

**Lesson 34
Day 4**

appearance	enhance	absence	reference
guidance	entrance	confidence	silence
intelligence	reliance	experience	residence
	grievance	patience	

A. Finish each list word.

1. ap_____   2. s_____

3. ent_____   4. e__h_____

5. gu_____   6. gri_____

7. i_____   8. r__s_____

9. r__f_____   10. c_____

11. r__l_____   12. p_____

13. ex_____   14. a___s_____

B. Copy the following sentence. **It was nice for Dan to finally experience total silence at the entrance of his residence.**

_____

_____

_____

_____

C. Write the definition from Day 1 for the list word **patience**.

_____

_____

Date: _____

Lesson 34 - Day 5, Final Test   Correction Area: _____

1. _____   _____
2. _____   _____
3. _____   _____
4. _____   _____
5. _____   _____
6. _____   _____
7. _____   _____
8. _____   _____
9. _____   _____
10. _____   _____
11. _____   _____
12. _____   _____
13. _____   _____
14. _____   _____

Carry-over Words: Correction Area:

1. _____   _____
2. _____   _____
3. _____   _____
4. _____   _____

**Lesson 35
Day 1**

Words with **Greek** and **Latin** prefixes and suffixes

1. **Review Your List Words**

    Look at the list words below and read each word to yourself. Then review each definition.

    Below is a list of the **Greek** and **Latin prefixes** and **suffixes** used in this lesson along with their meanings.

bio = life	**port** = carry	**bi** = two	**tele** = from afar
ex = out	**photo** = light	**logy** = study of	**trans** = across
geo = earth	**auto** = self	**cycle** = circle	**ion** = state of being
ped = food	**mobile** = move	**able** = able to	**graphy** = write
graph = write	**act** = do	**en** = to cause to	**phone** = sound

List Words		**Definitions**
geology	*geology*	• The study of the history of the earth.
transport	*transport*	• To carry from one place to another.
biology	*biology*	• The study of living things.
export	*export*	• To sell abroad.
enact	*enact*	• The process of making something law.
automobile	*automobile*	• A self-propelled vehicle for transporting people or cargo.
photograph	*photograph*	• A picture taken with a camera.
autograph	*autograph*	• A person's own signature.
bicycle	*bicycle*	• A two-wheeled vehicle with pedals.
telephone	*telephone*	• A device which transmits and receives sounds over long distances.
portable	*portable*	• Easily carried about.
biography	*biography*	• A written account of another person's life.
action	*action*	• The state of acting or doing.
biped	*biped*	• An animal that has two feet.

2. **Take Your Pretest**

    Turn to the next page to the Pretest section and your teacher will ask you to write each list word one at a time.

Date: _____

Correction Area:

1. _____   _____

2. _____   _____

3. _____   _____

4. _____   _____

5. _____   _____

6. _____   _____

7. _____   _____

8. _____   _____

9. _____   _____

10. _____   _____

11. _____   _____

12. _____   _____

13. _____   _____

14. _____   _____

Carry-over Words: Correction Area:

1. _____   _____

2. _____   _____

3. _____   _____

4. _____   _____

Lesson 35 Day 2

geology	export	autograph	biography
transport	enact	bicycle	action
biology	automobile	telephone	biped
	photograph	portable	

Latin and Greek Origins:

bio = life	**port** = carry	**bi** = two	**tele** = from afar
ex = out	**photo** = light	**logy** = study of	**trans** = across
geo = earth	**auto** = self	**cycle** = circle	**ion** = state of being
ped = food	**mobile** = move	**able** = able to	**graphy** = write
graph = write	**act** = do	**en** = to cause to	**phone** = sound

A. Show the parts that make up each list word, and then write the list word:

1. _____ + _____ = g_____

2. _____ + _____ = e_____

3. _____ + _____ = a_____gr_____

4. _____ + _____ = a_____mo_____e

5. _____ + _____ = biol_____

6. _____ + _____ = b__p_____

7. _____ + _____ = e_____rt

8. _____ + _____ = po_____

9. _____ + _____ = ph_____

10. _____ + _____ = b_____gr_____y

11. _____ + _____ = t_____t

12. _____ + _____ = b__c_____

13. _____ + _____ = ac_____

14. _____ + _____ = te_____

**Lesson 35
Day 3**

geology	export	autograph	biography
transport	enact	bicycle	action
biology	automobile	telephone	biped
	photograph	portable	

A. Read each clue. Write a list word in the blanks to answer each clue. Read down the shaded cells to find the answer to the question asked. Write the answer to the question in the spaces provided.

1. State of acting or doing.

2. Study of life.

3. Study of earth's land.

4. Easily carried about.

5. To make a bill law.

6. Has two feet.

7. To carry from one place to another.

8. A camera takes this.

9. One's own signature.

10. Transmits sound.

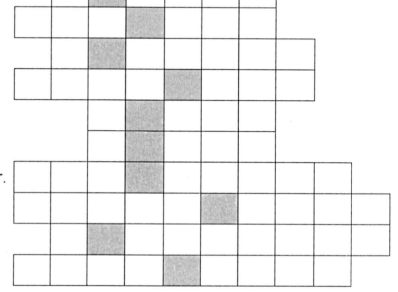

"Bobby was doing great as a janitor; he was..."

Answer: ____ ____ ____ ____ ____ ____ ____ ____   ____ ____.

B. Copy the following sentence. **We took a photograph of the action when the bicycle raced the automobile.**

_____

_____

_____

_____

_____

Lesson 35
Day 4

geology	export	autograph	biography
transport	enact	bicycle	action
biology	automobile	telephone	biped
	photograph	portable	

A. Draw a line to connect each list word with its definition.

geology   A picture taken with a camera.

transport   An animal with two feet.

biology   A written account of another person's life.

biography   The state of acting or doing.

enact   A person's signature.

automobile   Easily moved about.

action   The study of the history of the earth.

photograph   A two-wheeled vehicle with pedals.

autograph   The study of living things.

bicycle   To sell abroad.

biped   The process of making something law.

telephone   An engine driven vehicle.

portable   A device which transmits and receives sounds over long distances.

export   To carry from one place to another.

B. Write the definition from Day 1 for the list word **telephone**.

_____

_____

_____

Lesson 35 - Day 5, Final Test   Correction Area:

1. _____   _____

2. _____   _____

3. _____   _____

4. _____   _____

5. _____   _____

6. _____   _____

7. _____   _____

8. _____   _____

9. _____   _____

10. _____   _____

11. _____   _____

12. _____   _____

13. _____   _____

14. _____   _____

Carry-over Words: Correction Area:

1. _____   _____

2. _____   _____

3. _____   _____

4. _____   _____

**Lesson 36
Review
Day 1**

Review of words with vowel blends
oi, oy, ou, and ow

List Words

choice	annoy	tour	borrow
heroic	destroy	overflow	outgrown
moisten	voyage	astound	toward
	double	allowed	

A. Write the list word that matches each brief definition.

1. To irritate or bother.

    _____

2. To grow too large for something.

    _____

3. Twice the number.

    _____

4. To do away with or damage.

    _____

5. To permit or allow to happen.

    _____

6. To take and return something.

    _____

7. To make slightly wet.

    _____

8. To move in the direction of.

    _____

9. Confusion that amazes.

    _____

10. Traveling for pleasure.

    _____

11. Being courageous or fearless.

    _____

12. To flow out of the top.

    _____

13. A long journey by water.

    _____

14. Choosing something.

    _____

Lesson 36
Review
Day 2

Date: _____

Review of words that mean **fun**

List Words

excitement	game	merry	frolic
amusement	joke	comedy	pleasure
play	humor	funny	recreation
	enjoyable	entertain	

A. Finish the crossword puzzle.

Across:
4. To say something funny.
5. A feeling of enjoyment.
7. A funny play or movie.
9. Active in a joyful manner.
10. To be playful.
13. To be entertained by something.
14. To do something that captures interest or amuses.

Down:
1. To be agitated or excited.
2. Able to see amusing quality.
3. To be full of joy or delight.
6. A relaxing time for fun.
8. Activity that gives pleasure.
11. A fun activity with rules.
12. Something that causes laughter.

B. Write the definition from Day 1 for the list word **entertain**.

_____

_____

_____

Lesson 36
Review
Day 3

Review of words with the
suffixes **ity** and **ive**

List Words

equality	selective	electricity	productive
originality	availability	superiority	destructive
creative	density	supportive	objective
	detective	humidity	

A. Underline the list words in the following sentences.

1. Equality was very important to all in attendance.
2. The originality of the painting was astounding.
3. The fire was extremely destructive to the forest.
4. The objective of the class was to learn ballet.
5. The team worked together to be productive.
6. The water turned the turbine, which made electricity.
7. The humidity in the air made us sweat.
8. Barbara was very selective in choosing a new car.
9. The detective was very diligent in finding the clues.
10. We were all very supportive of bringing items to the bake sale.
11. Grandma was very creative when she made the colorful pillow.
12. The availability of space for the party needed to be confirmed.
13. The density of the bugs in the room was horrible.
14. The superiority of the perfect diamond was obvious.

B. Correctly write the above list words in the order they were found.

1. _____   2. _____

3. _____   4. _____

5. _____   6. _____

7. _____   8. _____

9. _____   10. _____

11. _____   12. _____

13. _____   14. _____

Date: _____

Review of words with the suffixes **ence** and **ance**

List Words

appearance	enhance	absence	reference
guidance	entrance	confidence	silence
intelligence	reliance	experience	residence
	grievance	patience	

A. Find and circle each list word in the puzzle below.

```
E  L  E  W  F  F  R  E  F  E  O  I  J  E  G
I  C  K  C  R  B  C  E  N  H  N  N  P  C  U
T  E  N  M  N  N  K  T  S  T  T  E  D  N  I
R  O  D  A  E  E  R  N  E  I  C  K  D  A  D
M  S  J  S  I  A  I  L  F  N  D  U  E  H  A
N  L  B  A  N  L  L  R  A  Z  D  E  C  N  N
D  A  P  C  S  I  E  V  E  D  V  K  N  E  C
O  T  E  W  G  F  E  R  V  P  D  H  E  C  E
G  B  T  E  V  I  A  A  J  S  X  H  D  T  E
E  C  N  A  R  A  E  P  P  A  Y  E  I  B  F
Z  C  F  G  E  C  N  E  I  T  A  P  F  L  X
E  S  I  L  E  N  C  E  X  X  K  Z  N  U  A
R  E  F  E  R  E  N  C  E  V  R  K  O  L  V
W  G  T  Q  S  G  G  A  H  Q  I  O  C  L  Z
C  V  C  W  E  W  S  F  R  X  Z  J  S  P  S
```

Date: _____

Review of words with **Greek** and **Latin prefixes** and **suffixes**

List Words

geology	export	autograph	biography
transport	enact	bicycle	action
biology	automobile	telephone	biped
	photograph	portable	

A. Unscramble the following list words.

aoncti

1._____

bphyiogra

3. _____

ptrobale

5. _____

pothoprgah

7. _____

tarnsorpt

9. _____

boilgoy

11. _____

atuorgpha

13. _____

bpide

2._____

gloegoy

4._____

teelhpone

6._____

encta

8._____

eortxp

10._____

atoumoible

12._____

bciyelc

14._____

<<Intentionally left blank>>